What About Me?

Growing Up with a
Developmentally
Disabled Sibling

If I Could Explain It

Brother
Sister,
Is who you are
To one another.

You eat waffles and macaroni
Together,
Put your pajamas on
At the same time.
And I scold you both,
Although for different reasons.
Different universes.

I wish I could explain to you
My "pre- two" daughter
Why your brother doesn't look at you
Very often (or hug you back when you playfully hug him.)
Doesn't say as many words as you,
Doesn't say your name (or his).

The months have passed
Of your innocent sister embrace
And giving him little blocks, cars
That may never be returned.

If you knew it was called autism,
Would it make a difference
That too often I've told you
"Your brother wants to be left alone now."

Today,
As you both sit on the couch together
Both separate in the same room
Playing different games,
I see
A toddler girl
Who has learned to ignore
What she cannot compete with
Anymore this afternoon,
A silence
Bigger than the absence of words.

From *Seasons of Love, Seasons of Loss*
by Connie Post, 1991

What About Me?

Growing Up with a Developmentally Disabled Sibling

Bryna Siegel, Ph.D.
and
Stuart Silverstein, M.D.

Foreword by
Glen R. Elliott, M.D., Ph.D.

PERSEUS PUBLISHING
Cambridge, Massachusetts

Library of Congress Cataloging-in-Publication Data

Siegel, Bryna.
    What about me? : growing up with a developmentally disabled
sibling / Bryna Siegel and Stuart Silverstein ; foreword by Glen
Elliott.
        p.   cm.
    Includes bibliographical references (p.   ) and index.
    ISBN 0-306-44650-2
    1. Developmentally disabled children--Family relationships.
2. Brothers and sisters--Psychology.   I. Silverstein, Stuart
II. Title.
HV891.S55 1994
362.1'968--dc20   94-99
                                                         CIP

Perseus Publishing books are available at special discounts for bulk
purchases in the U.S. by corporations, institutions, and other organizations.
for more information, plaese contact the Special Markets Department at the
Perseus Books Group, 11 cambridge Center, Cambridge, MA 02142, or call (800)
255-1514 or (617) 252-5298, or e-mail j.mccrary@perseus books. com.

ISBN 0-7382-0630-x

Published by Perseus Publishing
A Member of the Perseus Books Group

An Insight Book

Printed in the United States of America

To my family, in order of appearance:
Alyssa, David, and Daniel

—B. S.

DEEDS
Kind Hearts of the Gardens.
Kind Words are the Roots.
Kind thoughts are the Flowers.
Kind Deeds are the Fruits.
Take care of your Garden
and keep out the Weeds;
Fill it with Sunshine,
Kind words and Good Deeds.

—Anonymous

To the memory of my grandmother,
Sadie Shelibovsky, for whom our
family was her garden

—S. S.

Foreword

Those unfamiliar with the topic may wonder why someone is publishing a book about the impact a developmentally delayed child can have on family life in general and on that child's brothers or sisters in particular. Even the briefest reflection underscores the inevitability of such effects as one considers the special needs of such children both in the home and outside it. Is it not then reasonable to assume that research about and resources for siblings of children with autism, mental retardation, and other severe developmental disorders abound? Reasonable, perhaps; but incorrect.

Not so many years ago, the fate of children with severe delays of any kind was quite different than it is today. In the United States, as recently as the 1950s, such children were institutionalized almost as soon as they were identified and spent their lives hidden away from society. Usually, the resulting hole within the family, if acknowledged at all, was referred to obliquely, with a sense of shame and guilt. Siblings were apt to have only the vaguest notion about what happened to such a brother or sister.

As societal perceptions about the potential of developmentally delayed individuals to lead productive lives changed, so too did the expectations about family involvement in their care. Now, the vast majority of these children stay in the home at least through their adolescent years. Few of us formally train for the rigors of parenthood, but the need for training is nowhere more apparent than for parents with a "special-needs" child. They typically must become expert in marshalling the array of in-home, school, and social services their child may need, usually without any relief in other areas of their personal and professional lives. The mental and physical energy required can be enormous, as can the sheer time commitment.

Through the 1960s and 1970s, parents and social systems in the United States created totally new beliefs about children with developmental delays. A part of that change involved absolving parents of blame for their child's condition and replacing it with a sense of responsibility for their daily care. During that time, it is perhaps not surprising that the greatest attention was given to the likely gains for the child, rather than to the possible costs of such interventions.

After several decades of experience, it seems important to look more broadly at the consequences of the marked changes that have occurred in the care of children with severe developmental delays. Bryna Siegel and Stuart Silverstein make a major contribution to this task by exploring the varied ways in which children are affected by and cope with having a brother or sister who is delayed. They especially are to be congratulated for doing so in a way that provides a balanced survey of the kinds of situations, good and bad, that arise and the many factors that can influence outcomes.

This book will be of interest to parents, siblings, and professionals who work with children with chronic illnesses of any kind. It offers insights into some of the inevitable strains and stresses that the care of a child with severe delays can impose on any family while highlighting sources of support that can help ease the burden. Moreover, the stories told in this volume once again emphasize the diverse ways in which we human beings—child and adult alike—respond to and deal with the trials and tragedies of life.

GLEN R. ELLIOTT, M.D., Ph.D.

Associate Professor and Director
Child and Adolescent Psychiatry
University of California, San Francisco

Acknowledgments

This book has been an opportunity to synthesize many informal observations I've had the opportunity to make over the last ten years while working with families with developmentally disabled children. I am often asked how I manage to continue spending day after day as the person who tells families that their baby will never be normal. It is an incredibly painful task. I draw the energy that sustains me in this work from the dignity, strength, and spirit of the families who have to rise to meet this unexpected challenge. The families written about here are composites of many I've known. I hope those who recognize themselves will feel I've done the right thing by sharing a piece of their experience in a way that I hope will benefit other families. I thank them all.

I also thank my own quite blended family: my husband, David; my daughter, Alyssa; and my stepson, Dan. As a person who grew up without a brother or sister at home, I've learned a lot about families and siblings by watching us all in action.

B.S.

* * * * *

I would like to acknowledge the adult siblings who volunteered to be interviewed for this book. My contact with them was not only informative but healing. I learned a lot about myself and my own experience through our conversations.

I would also like to acknowledge my wife, Guita, and my stepdaughter, Isra, for providing the time and space to write and think.

I also acknowledge my parents, Beverly and Richard, for doing their very best. My relationship with them becomes more important each year. Further, I thank my sister as well as my parents for allowing me to include our story so that others may benefit.

S.S.

Contents

Chapter 3

*A Family's Adjustment to a Developmentally
Disabled Child* 39

Chapter 4

*Cultural, Religious, and Educational Factors Influencing
Family Adjustment* 71

The Introduction and Chapters 2, 3, and 4 were written by Dr. Siegel; Chapter 1 was written by Dr. Silverstein; Chapters 5, 6, 7, 8, 9, and 10 were written by Dr. Silverstein and Dr. Siegel; the Appendixes were written by Dr. Siegel and Dr. Silverstein. Chapter 11 was written by Michael A. Zatopa, Esq.

What About Me?

Growing Up with a Developmentally Disabled Sibling

Introduction

Personal and Clinical Perspectives on Siblings of Developmentally Disabled Children and Adults

The purpose of this book is to help families with developmentally disabled children to head off problems that may occur, to understand problems that already exist, and to work toward solutions to their problems. We are especially concerned about the *siblings* of those with developmental disabilities. A main focus of this book is on adult siblings looking back on their childhood and trying to sort out how their past experiences have influenced their current lives. Having a developmentally disabled child puts an extra burden on any family, and everyone feels it. During the growing-up period, the other siblings are children, too. Because as children they are less mature—less well organized emotionally and cognitively than adults—it can be even more difficult for siblings to muster the resources needed to cope with having a disabled child in the home.

Although not every family with a developmentally disabled child has problems as a result, the information offered in this book is intended for those who feel their experience has in some ways been darkly colored by having a disabled sibling. This book is for those who wish to examine the stressful aspects of their personal experiences with their sibling and with their family, and who want a better understanding of those experiences. Many parents worry about how well their nonhandicapped children are really doing, as they watch them try to live a "normal" life in parallel with the more atypical experiences they have with their mentally retarded brother or sister. We hope we can give some insight to such parents.

We also hope the book will be a resource for therapists and case managers who work with the families of developmentally disabled children, or with the developmentally disabled themselves.

In this book, we use terms like *mental retardation, retarded, developmentally disabled, developmental disorder, handicapped,* and *special needs* rather interchangeably. We refer to the brothers and sisters of affected children as *nonhandicapped siblings, nondisabled siblings,* or *normal children* (although we know that no child is entirely normal, all of the time). Similarly, we speak of *mentally retarded children* as well as of *children with mental retardation,* although we acknowledge that, as those who prefer the latter term point out, all children are children first, and that *mental retardation* is just one term that describes such children. We select none of these terms to create a stigma, and we apologize to any readers to whom one of these terms may be particularly less desirable than another.

Most of the information we provide is clinical—observations about particular families and about the prototypical patterns of functioning of nonhandicapped siblings that may create short-term or long-term problems for them. The approach we take stands, therefore, in contrast to empirical research studies that have sought to understand trends, group differences, and general principles relating to siblings of the developmentally disabled. By providing a more qualitative analysis of this area, we hope to help individuals who may recognize parts of themselves, their families, or issues they have faced.

In this book, we place special emphasis on autism, which is a neurologically based disability like mental retardation, and which is accompanied by mental retardation in the majority of cases. Autism often provides a particularly poignant example of many of the issues we raise because autistic children give so little back to their siblings and parents compared with children who have many other mental retardation syndromes. We often focus on autism as an example because our personal and clinical experiences have largely been with autistic children and their families. In fact, it is the convergence of our personal and clinical perspectives that has brought us to writing this book together. Stu Silverstein is today a pediatrician; he grew up with a mentally retarded autistic brother. Bryna Siegel directs a university clinic for children with autism and related disorders and does clinical research on children and families that come to her clinic. In writing this book, we wished to meld Stu Silverstein's self-help perspective as an adult sibling of a developmentally disabled individual with Bryna Siegel's perspective as someone who has the opportunity to observe many brothers and sisters of developmentally disabled children in action with their siblings and parents.

This book takes a psychodynamic perspective, encouraging the reader to reexamine his or her own feelings and beliefs about being a sibling of a developmentally disabled individual. Such an experience is different for each person, the key ingredients being personality, experience, the handicapped sibling's personality and specific disability, and the family's structure and its social supports. We cover several stages of development and the problems that may be associated with each for the nondisabled sibling. We outline the prototypical use of coping mechanisms and the personality types that often emerge from families with developmentally disabled children. There may still be a significant need to rethink and emotionally rework beliefs and feelings from childhood and adolescent problems associated with the handicapped sibling. We also cover aspects of adulthood that present continuing challenges for the adult sibling of a developmentally disabled brother or sister, such as concerns about forming one's own family, and about facing the various emotional, practical, and legal roles one may be asked to take (or may be handed) for the long-term care of an adult disabled sibling. We provide suggestions for positive coping through materials for the examination of one's feelings about oneself and his or her sibling, and we also provide concrete advice on what one needs to know about the options for long-term physical and financial oversight.

We urge the reader to open the Pandora's box of childhood and see what is really in it. For many, the experience of having a disabled sibling has forged strength. We hope that the reader may gain some insight and grow stronger as we share some personal experiences, as well as the experiences of the many families we have come to know and respect.

Chapter 1

A Personal Story

This chapter is written by Stuart Silverstein. As the brother of an autistic man, he gives his personal recounting of having grown up with a developmentally disabled sibling.

As I write this chapter, it has been a year since I last saw my brother Marc. In the past, a visit home always meant that I would see him without making any special effort, but things have changed since he was placed in a home for developmentally delayed adults. Even my calls home are no longer interrupted by his picking up the extension and repeating the same phrase: "Buy underwear, buy underwear . . . ." A special effort is required to speak to my brother now, and our conversation will never go beyond simple sentences: "What did Marc eat for lunch today? Tuna? Was it good?" For the first time since childhood, I am faced with the reality of his condition. He will always be this way.

Emotionally, I have to face the fact that he is autistic, something I always knew intellectually but never came to grips with. He will always be like a four-year-old: cute and funny at times, annoying and frustrating at others, living in his own world. I love him and I suspect he loves me, but his development ended while mine has continued. Each visit home, whether I see him or not, will reinforce this knowledge, eroding my denial.

In Marc's eyes, he has gone to "sleep-away school," something he saw our sister and me do when we went to college. Perhaps, at twenty-six, it was time for him to move on as well. It is always sad to watch your children leave home, but that sadness is always tempered with the knowledge that independence is a sign of growth. Not so with my brother Marc. Our sense of loss is compounded by guilt and the nagging question of whether this was the right move, or whether we are just rationalizing to allow ourselves the easy way out. Above all, it opens up old wounds.

Surely this was the best and probably the only possible move for everyone in our family, including Marc. After all, his needs are provided for, and my parents finally have some time to themselves after twenty-six years of raising him. However, emotions always have a way of lagging behind logic. The feelings that accompany sending your full-grown son to an adult home range from elation and relief to guilt and anguish. In practical terms, my parents' life has now become infinitely easier, but the void they feel is also immense. Whenever my father sees Sesame Street, my brother's favorite show, he cries. Taking care of my brother occupied my parents' time and energy, and like an old shoe, it felt comfortable. A new shoe always feels uncomfortable at first.

During my last two trips to New York, there were numerous reasons why I couldn't make the trip to Long Island to see Marc: my stay was short, there were friends to visit, weddings to prepare for. I think it is ambivalence—and my reluctance to open old wounds—that has really prevented me from making the trip. To see him in the home, I will have to face up to the fact that his life is severely limited, and that he will always be dependent on others. How could I then turn around and enjoy my life, after leaving him behind? As long as I don't have an image of his real world, I can envision it as being as pleasant as I want. I was four when the severity of his condition was unfolding. At this crucial juncture, when I needed my parents for my own growth and development, they were drowning emotionally while the severity of Marc's condition was becoming apparent.

My father recalls watching us sleep at night: "You looked so much alike, you could pass for twins—that is, until you woke up. Then the difference was jolting." Indeed, at first glance, we could pass for twins; we were only sixteen months apart and frequently wore matching outfits.

My parents discovered Marc's condition gradually, unlike a physical or medical disability, which hits you all at once. But, for me, he was always disabled. I recall coming late to kindergarten every Wednesday because we had to take my brother to the hospital for his weekly evaluation. Later on, when asked the simple question, "What grade is your brother in?" I either had to lie or divulge something about myself that I was unprepared to reveal. At a time when blending in was the most important thing in my life, I stood out.

I would frequently wait by the elevator after school, waiting for my mother and my brother to return from the "hospital," where Marc was to be seen by the doctors. My seven-year-old mind figured that they were going to find out what was wrong with him, give him some medicine, and cure him, just as they did for me when I was sick. I fantasized that one day he would walk out of the elevator talking normally. In many ways, this is the picture my parents saw, and I was only reflecting their attitude. They were going to the authorities for the answers and the cure. They had followed all the rules and received good prenatal care, so there must be an explanation for their being dealt this bad hand. They would often return late from the clinic where he was being evaluated, and a neighbor would look after me. After spending the day with the doctors, going over the dismal prognosis, my mom returned emotionally and physically spent. My dad would return from work as a spotter in a dry-cleaning store to receive the depressing news. There was little, if any, room left over for me and my problems. I was an emotional orphan.

I don't think I realized the sadness and depression my parents were experiencing at the time, although I could sense that something was wrong. They took it hard when Marc couldn't attend school with the rest of the children his age. My mother often told me how devastated she felt bringing Marc home after they had dropped me off at school. Watching other children his age getting dropped off with their siblings reinforced this pain. She frequently wore sunglasses in public to hide her swollen eyes.

Confused, I asked a lot of questions, but nobody told me what was going on—partly to "protect me," but mostly because my parents were just as perplexed as I was. "Don't worry, he's just slow, and he'll outgrow it"; "You're imagining things"; "We see this all the time"; "I, too, was a slow learner"—these are some of the answers pediatricians often give to soften the blow or to make themselves feel better. The doctors' smoke screen of professional rhetoric didn't satisfy my parents' need for answers, or at least their need for explanations and reassurance.

I can't imagine how difficult it must have been for them. Giving birth to a handicapped child shakes one to the core. It is the thing feared by most expectant parents. Once they realize that there is a "problem," their first question is *why?*. Unfortunately, there rarely is an answer. It is then the job of the health professional to share in their disappointment and helplessness.

Whenever a child is ill, parents tend to blame themselves. The tendency toward self-blame is even stronger with the birth of a handicapped child, especially when the cause is unknown. The imagination has a field day: "It was the antihistamines I took," "that one glass of wine," "I watched too many game shows." Parents want an explanation, any explanation, even that it was their fault. Then, at least, it wouldn't be a chance occurrence. They would be left with a feeling of control and could take steps in the future to prevent it. It is the job of the psychologist or psychiatrist to reassure the parents that they are not to blame.

Unfortunately, with autism this was not the case. On the contrary, parents were the "official" cause of the disease. In the early 1960s, when my brother's condition was first discovered, it was considered a "psychogenic" disease. Thus, the cause of the disease was the environment in which he lived, that is, the family.

In the case of autism, the blame was placed squarely with the mother. The mothers of autistic children were termed *refrigerator mothers*. The autistic child's inability to relate appropriately to the outside world was believed to be the result of the mother's coldness and inability to provide a warm, nurturing environment in which the child would develop. This was indeed the most widely held explanation in the field of psychiatry. The treatment of choice was removal of the child from the pathogenic household and placement in foster care. Psychiatrists never explained why this environment was okay for the other sibs in the family. Why weren't they autistic, too? This explanation is the worst case scenario for parents: Their child has a disorder and they are the cause. I can't imagine what my parents thought and felt.

My father recalls being asked "How is your sex life?" by the psychiatrist handling Marc. My father just turned around and left the room in disgust. I can understand why my parents have been reluctant all these years to seek help in dealing with Marc. As a result of our not seeking help, we never acknowledged our vulnerability and hurt. I suspect many others have felt the same way. Fortunately, this approach has changed. Autism is no longer "blamed" on the mother. It is now considered primarily a disease with a biological basis, not a psychogenic disease. Unfortunately, traces of this view still remain: In certain circles of the psychiatric community, primarily the psychoanalytic circle, the psychological makeup of the parents is still seen as a contributing factor.

In reading through the essays and stories written by other siblings of handicapped children, I see a similar tendency toward a denial of their feelings. Instead, they acknowledge the more positive emotions and experiences. They talk about their "special" brother, how he has brought the family close together, makes them laugh, and makes them so much more compassionate. Everyone then steps back and says, "Now, isn't that nice. His sister has adjusted so well to the situation." I see very little acknowledgment of the darker emotions. What about the hurt, anger, frustration, and resentment that I know exists? I would gladly exchange some of my compassion and sensitivity for a "normal" Marc. We siblings are not supposed to feel angry and resentful. Such feelings imply selfishness and insensitivity. But in not acknowledging these feelings, we only feed into denial. Even the use of euphemistic terms like *exceptional family* or *special brother* is a subtle way of denying hurt feelings.

In the beginning, my denial was so strong that, when asked what impact Marc has had on my life, I proudly claimed, "Since Marc was around all my life, and I have never known any different: no impact!" I then explained how much more sensitive to others I am because of Marc. I think that, as a child, I was perceptive enough to realize that this was what others were comfortable hearing. An expression of my true feelings would have been too overwhelming for all concerned.

Even as I sit writing these words, a part of me wonders whether Marc really has had an impact on my emotional health or whether I am just wallowing in self-pity. After all, there are many others with misfortunes greater than mine. To complain about mine *still* makes me feel guilty. I can still hear my parents, in their own anguish and frustration, yelling at my sister and me, "Be thankful it's not you." Sometimes, I do think, "My God, it really could have been me. I could be the one in the home. What do I have to complain about?" However, many others have not had to grow up putting their needs second. They didn't have to suppress their anger when they came home to discover three of their LP records smashed. They played carelessly, as children were meant to. They didn't have to keep an "eye out" for their brother and accept blame when he "acted out." It is no wonder that, by my early twenties, I already felt burnt out.

I wonder how I could have denied all this. Yet, while I was growing up, denial was the rule, the protective armor. My mother is still in a state of denial about the severity of Marc's condition. To some extent, she is still waiting for him to improve, or for some cure to come along.

There were much chaos and much physical violence in my growing up, often because of something Marc had done or reacted to. These, too, were denied or played down. I remember my parents saying to me in the midst of utter chaos and fighting, "What problem? Do you think this doesn't go on in other families? They just don't talk about it." To discuss the situation with anybody was a betrayal of family loyalty. I'm sure this sort of thing *did* go on in other families, but it was the exception, not the rule. It was after I had left for college and had placed some distance between my family and myself that I realized my family had problems beyond the norm. Once I had "discovered" therapy, I often begged them to go as well. Unfortunately, their first relationship with psychologists and psychiatrists had been adversarial, not collaborative. Therefore, they refused to obtain counseling. Given what they had been through, I can't say that I blamed them.

Denial leaves you out of touch with your true feelings, incapable of finding the necessary energy to deal with the situation at hand. You end up mistrusting your own intuition in important situations and heading down the path to insecurity, low self-esteem, and depression. You are left a legacy of helplessness.

Much has been written about the adult children of alcoholics (ACOAs). Many of their problems as adults stem from having grown up in a family where someone's "behavioral problem" exerted a negative influence. In order to cope, they used a lot of denial and accommodation to the needs of the alcoholic parent. In these families, poor coping and interpersonal skills are developed in childhood. ACOAs, despite appearances, frequently experience low self-esteem, guilt, and bouts of depression. This description of ACOAs struck a resonant chord with me. I recognized my sister and myself in the description of their backgrounds and their emotional state as adults. This discovery reinforced my growing acknowledgment of Marc's impact on our lives, something I had previously denied.

Although there was no alcoholism in our family, conflict and tension were common, and we were dependent on the unpredictable behavior of a family member. I decided to do some reading on the subject of ACOAs. It talked about the disease "codependency," born of having to meet the needs of another at one's own expense. This certainly was our case growing up with Marc. Many of our activities as a family were curtailed, and I was frequently responsible for looking after him.

The similarity between ACOAs and my sister is even more striking, and it was in watching her come of age that I really began to think about the impact Marc has had on our lives. My sister Stacey, who is nine years younger than I, served as a mirror to my past, a not-so-gentle reminder of how things had been for me. I remember an early-morning phone call from my parents, asking me to explain to my sister why she must agree to Marc's going along with them to the open house at the college that had just accepted her. I didn't want to be placed in that position. I understood how she felt. She didn't want to have to explain his behavior to anyone. This was her event and she didn't want to share it with our brother. I felt that my parents should have made other arrangements to accommodate her. The crises and conflicts in her life have forced me to face similar ones in my own life. With each phone call, I am dragged back down, confronting issues I thought I had either resolved or buried.

When Stacey was born, the prospect of having a sister was very exciting. I never consciously thought about the possibility of another handicapped sibling, but that specter certainly hung over my parents' heads during those early days of her life. Stacey was the "gamble" my parents took after having Marc and the one miscarriage after him. Because Marc's diagnosis had been made gradually over time, they monitored Stacey's growth and development closely, checking for any subtle signs of delay.

I saw the process through the eyes of a ten-year-old. I watched Stacey's vain attempts to engage Marc in play and often wondered if this little girl knew that Marc was not "normal." It wasn't long before she took on the role of an older sibling, taking care of and watching out for him. This looked cute at first but was symbolic of things to come.

Today, her "sense of self" is a confused one. Making decisions and trusting her instincts are difficult. With all the chaos and disruption centering on Marc, how could they not be difficult? My brother's worsening behavior coincided with Stacey's adolescence, and our parents had very little reserve left over to deal with her "emotional turmoil." Her complaints about his walking around in his underwear, his going to the bathroom with the door open, or his tearing up her clothes were deemed selfish. If she didn't "understand," she was immature and ungrateful for being normal. She was expected to adapt to his behavior accordingly, something that required a maturity beyond her years. She was to be a "little adult," denied the carefree days of childhood and adolescence. Today she has finally begun to express her anger and resentment over the role she was forced to play. I am happy to see this reaction; it is the first step on the road to healing.

Certainly, in comparison to my brother's "problem," any complaints we had were trivial. The request for privacy may seem selfish compared to what's in store for my brother in his life. Nevertheless, such requests are important for healthy development, and most people take them for granted. Stacey recalls that, as a five-year-old, she returned from a birthday party with a balloon, which Marc grabbed and broke. She wondered for days whether her friends still had their balloons. Very little effort was made to console her; after all, it was only a balloon, but to a little girl a balloon can be the whole world.

It is easy to minimize the concerns of a small child. To do otherwise requires that extra effort of stepping into the child's world. This is a difficult task even under near-perfect conditions, one of the reasons child rearing is such a hard job. Add the burden of raising an autistic child, with his or her unpredictable outbursts and demands, and there is very little patience left over for the effective parenting of the rest of the children.

As a result, I feel guilty about being angry at my parents. Why? Because, despite their best efforts, things didn't turn out as well as they would have liked or expected. I even have some trouble putting these words on paper for fear of how my parents will feel reading them. My feelings are a mixture of forgiveness and understanding, as well as anger. They did their best to make us happy in a difficult set of circumstances that they were not prepared for. They would frequently replace our belongings that

Marc broke. I would then feel bad for them: Not only did they have to deal with their own anger and frustration, they had to appease us as well. No wonder they expected us to be more understanding.

With time, my mother grew more sympathetic to my sister and her needs, whereas my father's sympathies still lay more with my brother. This conflict placed a tremendous strain on our parents' relationship, the polarization consuming the few emotional resources they had left. Having moved out years earlier, I was capable of seeing both sides clearly. However, both sides were incapable of understanding and compromise. The arguments and fights would escalate, often into physical violence. When things got "out of hand," I was called in to talk to my sister. Conflict was the rule, and we all lost.

All the issues I describe above hold true for me as well, but to a lesser extent. I say to a lesser extent because of age and gender difference. For one thing, as he grew older, Marc's outbursts and behavior worsened, along with the "functioning" of our family. As a result, Stacey grew up in a more dysfunctional home than I did. It is one thing to be a fifteen-year-old boy with a thirteen-year-old brother who runs around the house flapping his arms and making odd sounds; your friends are less likely to be intimidated and stay away. It is another story if you are a fifteen-year-old girl, and your twenty-two-year-old brother behaves this way. Marc's behavior contributed to Stacey's shyness and her reluctance to make friends and invite them over while she lived at home. If you grow up with your needs and concerns trivialized by others, you begin to trivialize them yourself, automatically. It's a pattern that will follow you to adulthood.

There was always a sense of mourning and melancholy in the air when I was growing up. This, along with tension and chaos, was the norm. If things were going too well, I knew it was only a matter of time before they would fall apart again. This pattern of thinking has remained with me, and I have to remind myself consciously that happiness and peace, not despair and tension, are the natural feelings that we should experience.

I still wonder to what extent the screaming, yelling, and physical violence that occurred was a direct result of my brother. I have encountered families with an autistic member, in which none of this occurs. On the other hand, some families experience this type of activity—and there are no "abnormal" siblings. As is often the case, the truth probably lies somewhere in between. A tendency to resolve conflicts in this counterproductive way was a vulnerability that we as a family would have had in any case. Marc's extraordinary demands and our frustrations in dealing with him just exaggerated this tendency. Having an autistic child hits families at their weakest point and just makes it weaker. As a result, I have come to associate family life with chaos, pain, and stagnation. Although I crave intimacy like everyone else, I fear it as well and have managed to avoid it for the most part.

Lately, I have entertained the notion that Marc's condition may have influenced my career choice. I have denied this possibility in the past, as I did not consciously consider Marc's influence when applying to medical school. However, because a large percentage of the siblings of handicapped children do go into the helping professions, a closer look at my motivations has been warranted. This career choice makes sense, considering we have spent a lifetime meeting the needs of another, often at our own expense. All our lives, we have received praise and love from our parents for giving of ourselves—perfect training for one of the "helping professions." Although there is nothing inherently wrong with giving of ourselves to benefit others, the extreme form, as in anything else, can be self-destructive. I have come to realize that my career choice of pediatrics had a lot more to do with Marc than I initially realized or would admit. I now evaluate my motivation for doing things with this awareness.

In the past, I often wondered where my pain, insecurity, and chronic depression stemmed from. I even started to accept it as a part of life. "Everyone is depressed," my parents told me, but somehow I knew this couldn't be true. I assumed that my pain came from being a deep-thinking, sensitive person whose awareness left him vulnerable. But there have been many before me who were deeper thinkers, with greater awareness, who have led fulfilling, if not happy lives.

Living in the shadow of depression, chaos, and mourning hits you where you are most vulnerable. I have learned to recognize these weak points and to take steps to strengthen them. Above all, there is *always* hope. Perhaps those of us who find it so easy to put others' needs before our own need to put the Golden Rule in reverse: "Do unto yourself as you would do unto others." Over the years, through reading, therapy, and a great deal of patience from family and friends, my sister and I have recognized our vulnerable buttons and the motivations for our actions. As a result, we have found our lives dramatically improved.

Chapter 2

What Research Tells Us about the Brothers and Sisters of Developmentally Disabled Children

Relationships with siblings serve as a prototype for later relationships with other adults. Therefore, sibling relationships have been studied by child development researchers to learn how positive traits such as affiliativeness, altruism, and empathy, as well as negative traits such as self-centeredness and aggressiveness, may emerge. Much of what has been learned about sibling relationships comes from studying families in which none of the children has a disability. In these families, we have learned about characteristic differences in how young siblings relate to older ones, how brothers relate to sisters, and how all children come to realize that they must learn to share and cooperate. Benefits accrue from both getting and giving love, and typically, this is what happens in sibling relationships, along with learning to cope with the normal sibling frustrations of having to curb the impulse to want to be more important that one's brother or sister in the eyes of one's parents.

When there is a disabled sibling, this aspect of the family

system is out of whack. The usual rules about sharing parental attention and the rules about "If you're nice to him, he'll be nice to you" may or may not apply. Psychologists and psychiatrists who study family systems have given relatively little attention to what happens in these circumstances, compared to the amount of research that they have conducted on normal sibling relationships. However, since the late 1960s, a body of research has slowly built up that does address the experience of the siblings of developmentally disabled children. In one way or another, most of the studies have posed the question of whether growing up with a handicapped brother or sister is psychologically damaging. A few studies have asked the question the other way round and have speculated on whether growing up with a handicapped brother or sister may make one more resilient and more helpful to others.

In this chapter, we review research on the siblings of handicapped children and particularly on the circumstances in which a particular family with a particular constellation of family members and personalities may expect to encounter difficulties, and what these difficulties may be. We also direct the interested reader to key studies that highlight some of the main questions that have been asked and answered. Some of these studies are listed in the "For Further Reading" section at the end of this book.

The results of much of the research on the effects of having a developmentally disabled sibling show that many siblings do adjust well, but that in certain circumstances, some siblings and their families are clearly at risk, and do experience significant amounts of ongoing stress. We describe in this chapter the risk factors in such families, as well as protective factors that seem to ameliorate the problems that arise.

How Common Are Families with a Developmentally Disabled Member?

Casting the broadest net, the U.S. Department of Education notes that conditions that require some special educational services, at least for a while, affect approximately 10 percent of American children: This includes children with early developmental delays, language delays, learning disabilities, mental retardation, physical impairment, or sensory handicaps such as deafness or blindness. In most of these children, the handicaps are mild or transitory. For example, some children need infant stimulation because of premature birth, and some with mild lisps or stutters receive speech therapy but are cognitively quite normal. However, in any family where a child has a rough or a slow start in life, the family dynamics may subtly (or not so subtly) shift to favor the child with the disability, as has been shown in research on children born prematurely.

Relatively fewer families must cope with a child with mental retardation, but many people find the number surprisingly high. One recent survey estimated that about 2.5 percent of American children are classified as mentally retarded. This percentage translates into about 1 million children receiving special education for subnormal intellectual functioning or for a subnormal ability to do everyday things appropriate to that age. Given the average American family size, it is likely that somewhat more than 1 million children are siblings of mentally retarded children. And there are many more people who are the brothers and sisters of adults with mental retardation.

Among the 2 to 3 percent of the population who are mentally retarded, about two-thirds are mildly retarded and have good adaptive behavior; that is, they learn to help themselves quite adequately in everyday skills. Some of these individuals often blend into society with a little extra help from their families, special friends, and social service agencies. Others live independently but continue to draw heavily on family resources because they have a hard time keeping jobs, budgeting money, raising their own children, and just generally keeping out of trouble. They are at a higher risk than the general population of developing psychiatric disorders, and when they do, they are referred to as the *dually diagnosed,* that is, having both mental and psychiatric disabilities. The remaining third of the mentally retarded population (i.e., about 1 percent of the total population) have severe enough mental and adaptive disabilities to continue to need lifetime special care and supervision. Two-thirds of this 1 percent are moderately mentally retarded; that is, they grow up able to dress, feed, and toilet themselves independently, and to live according to simple routines in a sheltered environment like their own home, a group home, or an institution. About one-third of the 1 percent have severe or profound mental retardation; this is the group most likely to remain institutionalized as adults, and to have continued problems even in basic self-care. Depending on the family's beliefs, wishes, finances, and other variables, non-handicapped siblings may end up with some degree of lifetime responsibility for their handicapped brother or sister. This may mean as little as an annual hospital visit around Christmas or as much as full-time care in the adult sibling's home. Thus, a handicapped sibling may affect not only how his brothers and sisters were raised but also how his brothers and sisters are able to raise their children, especially if he or she comes to live with a non-handicapped sibling as an adult.

As we've stated, about 2.5 percent of children are classified as mentally retarded. These children (plus another half a percent of the population, for a total of 3 percent of all American children) receive ongoing special education for mental handicaps. In addition to the special-education population, who are the focus of what we are discussing here, there is an additional population of disabled children who are not mentally handicapped, but who do have permanent sensory handicaps or physical disabilities. Still more children have lifelong chronically debilitating physical diseases like cystic fibrosis, severe asthma, or insulin-dependent diabetes. Although we are focusing here on children with mental handicaps, children with physical disabilities have been shown to present to their families and siblings many of the same challenges in coping and caretaking as a child who has a developmental disability.

Although we have a general idea of how many disabled people there are, more fine-tuned breakdowns by disability or by family structure (like how many live in single-parent families and just what the divorce rate is in families with disabled children) are hard to come by. Part of the reason that such data are not readily available is that continuing stigma (as well as lack of funding) makes it difficult to count everyone. It is hard to get an accurate count of developmentally disabled infants and toddlers because there are some who family members or therapists feel will be "normal" soon, and they don't get counted because they don't come to the attention of treatment agencies. It is hard to count the developmentally disabled among school-aged children because definitions of mild mental retardation and learning disabilities may overlap, and some studies include one group but not the other. Some children who are developmentally disabled are counted among those primarily limited by sensory handicaps such as deafness or blindness. Developmentally disabled children also overlap with those primarily classified as having a physical disability like cerebral palsy or spina bifida. Counting cases of adults may offer even more problems, as the oldest of the developmentally disabled may never have received public services and may not be considered "retarded" by the family members who care for them.

Overall, the number of families touched by a developmentally disabled child or adult is high; perhaps as many as 3 million American children and adults have (or had) a mentally retarded brother or sister. All of these individuals are (or were, when growing up) at risk for the family coping problems we are discussing here. In children (and later, when they become adults), there is an effect on thinking and behavior as a result of having grown up with a handicapped sibling. This mark on personality arises, for better or worse, from the extent to which the normally developing sibling was expected to adjust his or her own behavior because of the disabled brother or sister. Adult siblings may still be grappling with feelings related to having had a mentally retarded sibling, especially as they begin to think about raising families of their own or to confront becoming their sibling's primary caretaker as their own parents grow older.

The "Labeling" of People with
Developmental Disabilities

Over the years, the terms we have used to describe people with developmental disabilities have continued to change; they are still changing. Changes in the nomenclature for developmental disorders reflect certain beliefs about what underlies the individual's problem, as well as what is the currently "politically correct" attitude toward such individuals. In the medical profession at the turn of the century, the degrees of mental retardation were referred to by words like *simpleton, idiot, moron,* and *imbecile.* Interestingly, although each of these words was used technically to refer to a certain degree of cognitive disability, all these words are now considered epithets for mentally retarded people.

Subsequent labeling focused on educability—a more upbeat note. Thus, individuals with mental retardation were classified into two broad groups: the *educable* mentally retarded (EMR) and the *trainable* mentally retarded (TMR). Still, the term *mentally retarded* sounded hopeless to many people because it encompassed those with mild cognitive impairments as well as individuals with more severe impairments. So today, many once classified as EMR are sometimes described as *learning-disabled* or *learning-handicapped* (LH) *students* rather than as EMR or even as mildly mentally retarded. The classification of TMR is now usually expressed as *severely handicapped* (SH) or as *moderately to severely mentally retarded.* These labels may help the reader "translate" into the language now in use, the terms that may have been applied to a brother or sister twenty or thirty years ago.

The current trend in labeling developmental disabilities is to steer away from terms that imply permanency like *minimal brain damage* (MBD), *brain-injured,* or *birth defects,* which were often used in the 1970s; instead, there has been a move toward more temporary-sounding terms like *developmentally delayed.* The parents of young children often feel that the term *developmentally delayed* implies that the child will eventually catch up, just as a "delayed" train eventually arrives. Professionals, by preferring the term *devel-*

opmentally delayed over the term *mental retardation,* may abrogate their responsibility to help families understand that they are dealing with a permanent disability in a child. When this happens, parents may find that they have set about a temporary reallocation of special attention to a "delayed" child in need of help to "catch up" and, before they know it, have made selective, preferential attention to the disabled child a permanent family lifestyle as the "delay" persists. If the parents see one of their children as developmentally "delayed," the siblings may be put on hold, waiting until the delayed child "arrives." Gearing up for a long-term adaptation to a stressor is very different from gearing up for a crisis or an acute stressor. A family that initially approaches a child's mental retardation as an acute stressor may be more susceptible to burnout.

A final interesting use of language in coping with mental retardation has been the recent introduction of terms like *developmentally different.* Yes, mentally retarded people are developmentally different. Unfortunately, the term also evokes associations such as "different but equal." But the "differences" between mentally retarded people and others put them at a definite disadvantage. To ignore that fact is to deny that it *is* more stressful to care for a child with special needs than it is to care for a child without a developmental disability.

In the context of a family, of course, a child is seldom referred to as "your autistic brother" or "your Down's sister." Usually, parents refer instead to the child's "problem," or "difficulty," or maybe even "disability." Quite often, the child's behavior that is symptomatic of the disorder is referred to in the same way as a personality trait: "He doesn't like to be touched," not "He doesn't like to be touched because he's autistic and he's tactilely defensive." Identifying the symptoms as part of personality may be helpful in normalizing their impact and seeing the child as a whole person. However, the lack of distinction between personality and symptoms makes it hard for a young sibling who is learning to deal with a handicapped brother or sister to know whether a bad reaction that he or she may have elicited is caused by the handicap or is genuinely his or her fault.

The Meaning of Sibling Relationships

As we stated at the outset, relationships between siblings serve as the prototype for all sorts of later consensual relationships. Benefits accrue from loving and being loved, and from learning how to cope with frustration and aggressive impulses. Dealing with their siblings is how most people learn to deal with their peers. Further, it is likely that the behavioral strategies that worked well in dealing with peers during childhood will mature into a style of handling other relationships in adulthood. Behavior that is commonly felt to have its roots in childhood, and especially in sibling relationships, includes competitiveness, altruism, nurturance, and aggressiveness.

Because sibling relations seem to bear on adult personality formation, sibling relationships in which one sibling was developmentally disabled were first studied from a psychoanalytic perspective. A 1972 study of Yale college students with disabled siblings showed that about half felt themselves to be the better for having grown up with a handicapped sibling; half felt they had been harmed. In that study, as well as in subsequent research, those who have reported feeling the better for the challenge of growing up with a handicapped sibling have tended to say that it has made them more altruistic, more empathetic, and more open to people with various sorts of difficulties. Many of the positive traits that are frequently mentioned are "externalizing"; that is, related to the ability to get along with others.

Those who report feeling harmed tend to report the opposite. They may feel that they have to fight off feelings of depression or self-worthlessness and lack an internal sense of self-validation. The negative traits are often "internalizing," and they may come from the lack of a sufficient number of opportunities as a child to feel special, worthwhile, important, or the center of positive attention. In addition, some studies have shown that feelings of altruism and feelings of depression do, in fact, sometimes coexist in the siblings of a disabled child. A recent study done in Toronto suggested that, although the siblings of autistic children were more helpful in caring for their brother or sister than were children whose sibling had no disability, these children tended also to feel depressed; half actually met the criteria for clinical depression. Adult siblings cite longer-term benefits more often than shorter-term ones. The positive consequences of being more altruistic and more helpful to others are valued traits that adult siblings can often identify in themselves. As children, many siblings of developmentally disabled brothers and sisters were so often told to defer their own needs so that their sibling could be attended to that putting themselves second became an unconditional part of how they related to others. Such siblings found that successfully deferring their own needs so that someone else's needs could be met became, instead, more a source of satisfaction than actually having their own needs met. Through this pattern arises an adult personality marked by altruism at best and a martyred attitude at worst. Although an adult sibling may actually be as gratified by a loved one's happiness as by his or her own happiness, as a child that person may not have been unambivalently self-sacrificing when asked to subvert his or her own needs to those of the sibling.

The general principle here is that childhood suffering sometimes produces a better adult with a greater sense of self-worth. Negative effects that adult siblings often cite have to do with unresolved difficulties first experienced as a child. Another negative feeling that has been often mentioned in a variety of studies is feeling neglected because one's own behavior did not seem to warrant as much parental interest as the handicapped sibling's behavior did. In some children—very young children, in particular—these feelings of neglect may result in acting out the symptomatic behavior of the handicapped children (e.g., spitting, if their sibling drools, and making weird noises instead of using words to indicate wants) in an attempt to provoke the same sympathetic parental response. Needless to say, this is seldom the result. Rather, the parents tend to become angry and exasperated, and to ignore the acting-out child. A young child may be quite confused about to why this should be so. After all, under normal circumstances, a younger child often imitates an older sibling's behavior because it has elicited positive parental attention. A very young child cannot easily tell that using words instead of grunting like his big brother is what his parents would prefer him to do, just because he has words and his older brother doesn't. What the young sibling learns is to resent what he believes is the inconsistency in the different standards of behavior set for him and for his brother.

Adult siblings also report resenting the handicapped child and then feeling guilty about their resentment. A double standard of behavior and being made to subvert one's needs produce anger directed not only at one's parents but also at the handicapped sibling, who is obviously part of the situation from which the nonhandicapped sibling comes out feeling the loser. As the sibling gets older, she intellectually realizes that some of her brother's behaviors are related to his handicap, and then feels guilty whenever she blames him for behavior that diminishes her share of parental attention.

Siblings may also feel embarrassed by their disabled brother's or sister's appearance or behavior. It is normal for late-latency and early-adolescent children (i.e., nine to twelve years old) to be so sensitive to the "right" and "wrong" way to act that even a normal younger sibling who violates these rules may be a source of embarrassment at a school function, a birthday party, or other public event. This type of response is naturally intensified when a sibling has an abnormal appearance or behaves in a way that other children haven't seen before. The preschool-age sibling does not realize what aspects of his handicapped sibling's behavior is considered abnormal by others; the latency-age child does know. Some latency-age siblings adapt with a counterphobic response, going out of their way to challenge other children who may call their sibling a "retard" or, as in a book about a boy and his autistic brother moving to a new neighborhood, making it a point to educate the other children about the fact that his brother is autistic (but can still hang out with them, kind of). Such a counterphobic response may be the most adaptive and practical way to cope when one considers all the more harmful ways of handling embarrassment (e.g., refusing to go anywhere with a sib and call ing the sib names himself). However, organizing those embarrassed feelings in order to produce an active, prosocial response takes a toll, too, and years later, resentment may still be harbored.

Another area in which siblings feel negatively affected by their handicapped brother or sister is in the differences in the normal levels of responsibilities and privileges. Several studies have measured this aspect by examining how much time nonhandicapped siblings spend in household chores and child care. Other studies have examined how often the family goes out together, and for what sorts of activities. Overall, families with disabled children do put more responsibilities on their nonhandicapped children and do go out less than matched control families. However, there is a lot of cultural and economic variation in how much time families allocate to chores and social activities, and so it is not possible to say that direct harm comes from the increased levels of responsibility and the decreased number of privileges that nonhandicapped siblings experience. It is clear, however, that the siblings accurately perceive that their family's home life is different from that of their peers.

Finally, another source of negative feelings is the sense that the members of one's family are alienated from each other. The cumulative effect of years of the parents' deferring normal social interactions with their nonhandicapped children in order to accommodate the handicapped child is that there may eventually be no tradition for getting along with one another, talking to one another, or finding ways to have fun together. This sense of alienation may be experienced more strongly in some families than in others.

Overall, the negative effects of having a handicapped sibling that have just been described may have varying degrees of impact on a sibling depending on her or his age, gender, and temperamental characteristics, and on the children's spacing and the family's size.

Factors Influencing Sibling Coping

The extent to which different siblings experience better and worse outcomes can be accounted for somewhat by such factors as birth order, family size, gender, parental coping, marital stability, social support, socioeconomic status, and cultural beliefs. In addition, individual personality differences and the defensive styles that arise from those personality differences are likely to play a significant role in one's adaptability to having a handicapped sibling. Another set of factors that has been less well studied is the characteristics of the developmentally disabled child himself or herself. It is known, in general, that the more severely mentally retarded the child is, the more difficulty everyone involved has.

Birth Order, Family Size, Child Spacing, and Gender

Research suggests that having a handicapped sibling is consistently more difficult for older sisters. Older sisters are more likely than older brothers, or younger siblings of either gender, to be recruited into caregiving tasks and are most often expected to function as second-string parents. At least one study has suggested that, after older sisters, younger brothers are the next most stressed. Younger brothers get less attention and, because they are boys, may get fewer chances to spend time with their parents by helping out in caregiving tasks that may be seen more as "girl" chores, such as helping to dress or feed the sibling.

Siblings who spend more time caring for their brother or sister naturally have less time to do other things. Some studies have shown that, when nondisabled siblings have markedly less time for the activities that their peers engage in, they are more likely to be resentful. This line of research makes apparent the importance for nonhandicapped siblings to have their own lives outside the family, commensurate with their age and interests. Going to Brownies or Girl Scouts, being on the soccer team, or being able to take karate classes is especially important if nonhandicapped siblings are to develop a sense that their lives are, in some ways at least, like everyone else's. Activities outside the home give children time to develop additional views of themselves that may counterbalance the less positive self-image caused by the difficult struggle at home to become an ever-better brother or sister to the handicapped sibling.

Often, research has not shown a clear effect of birth order alone, perhaps because distinctly different factors may make things worse for older or younger siblings in certain families: As older siblings grow up, they may be more apt to become alienated from the family because they may be seen as able to fend for themselves and as not needing the limited amount of care their parents can provide. Younger siblings may be at a disadvantage because they have never experienced a time when their parents were not mainly preoccupied with the handicapped sibling. Sometimes, the younger sibling is conceived before the parents know that the older child has a developmental problem. However, they may know by the time the younger child is born or is an infant. At that point, the younger child may be especially resented as an extra burden. Whenever a child comes after a disabled child, family stress tends to increase as there is less time left to care for babies who come subsequently.

Overall, girls tend to be more often affected negatively than boys. As mentioned above, girls are more often given a caregiving role. Becoming engaged in caregiving, although undoubtedly helpful to the parents, does not necessarily bring the hoped-for rewards: One of the studies which showed that siblings of handicapped children were more helpful than comparison children also showed that these children less often received positive feedback from their parents based on their helpfulness. On many occasions, I have seen a ten-year-old girl or eight-year-old boy fetch a bottle or favorite toy, offer food, or retrieve a wandering sibling—all without specific comment from the parents. Inevitably, these children look to see if they are going to be praised for their good deeds but seem to tolerate it fairly well when their helpfulness is taken for granted. However, if one of these same children should fail to be helpful when help is needed, the parents often seem quick to point out shortcomings in the nonhandicapped child's vigilance over his or her sibling's needs.

Girls and boys tend to handle their negative feelings about their siblings differently: Girls who fare badly because of having a handicapped sibling more often express their maladjustment through depression and anxiety. Boys, on the other hand, tend to direct their symptoms outward and show higher rates of aggressiveness and acting out. Some research has suggested that the likelihood of such symptoms in the siblings of handicapped children is increased if the mother is inconsistent, disorganized, or herself depressed and emotionally unavailable.

Another variable that some studies suggest affects adjustment is child spacing. Studies uniformly show that siblings who are close in age to the disabled sibling tend to experience more distress. The close-in-age sibling, especially if younger, tends to be particularly deprived of parental time and may be cared for by a variety of older siblings, relatives, and others who are helping out. A more psychological barrier that exists between close-in-age nonhandicapped siblings and their parents is that their developmental level is a concrete reminder of the degree and reality of their developmentally disabled sibling's shortcomings. When a twenty-month-old is starting to talk in short sentences and her three-year-old brother is still not making a sound, their parents can no longer hold on to the idea that some kids just talk late, and that the three-year-old is really OK. Similarly, when an older close-in-age child is nonhandicapped, the parents can easily remember that he walked at eleven months and ran at twelve months: the fourteen-month-old who still is uninterested in crawling seems more clearly to have a problem than when that fourteen-month-old is the firstborn. Some parents deny or minimize the accomplishments of the close-in-age nonhandicapped sibling, so that the contrast to the developmentally disabled child seems not to be so marked.

Sometimes, sibling adjustment is found to be more difficult when the siblings are the same sex than when they are of opposite gender. This finding probably has to do with how frustrating it is for the normal sibling not to be able to get an expected reaction from a same-sex sibling who, developmentally, should be almost a peer. Siblings who are closer in age tend to be more closely identified with one another's interests, values, and behavior. Researchers have speculated that life with a disabled sibling who is almost one's own age and of the same sex is probably harder because one would be more closely identified with the atypical behavior, and it would be more difficult to distance oneself from that sibling.

In addition to child spacing, family size is an important determinant of how well a child is likely to be able to cope. Just as being spaced farther away from the disabled sibling may be protective, coming from a large family is similarly protective. There is less one-to-one contact, less one-to-one comparison, and probably less attention to the foibles of the handicapped child than in families where the handicapped child is one of two or three siblings. I remember visiting a family where an autistic thirteen-year-old son was the youngest of five siblings (four boys and a girl) ranging up to twenty years old. When dinner was set out at that house, everyone sat down and, in a well-mannered way, inhaled the food, the autistic son included. When I commented on this to the boy's mother, she said her son had never been a picky eater or used poor table manners since the days when she'd send him to his room for fussing at the dinner table. He would return, and everything would be eaten. Larger families just don't have the time or space to create an entirely special world around a handicapped child. By and large, such families function to the child's advantage, helping her or him to function more in the mainstream. In addition, a number of studies have suggested that, in a larger family, the burden of raising the handicapped child can be more equally distributed than in smaller families so that no one sibling gets designated as the habitual second-string parent.

Research on Family Functioning

How well the family can function as a unit, or how well the parents functioned as a couple before the birth of the handicapped child, has been found to affect sibling adjustment to a developmentally disabled brother or sister. Important factors that have been examined in a number of studies include maternal psychiatric status, marital stability, and socioeconomic status. Virtually no research exists on cultural differences in adaptation to handicap, although in Chapter 4 some speculation on this subject based on clinical experiences is presented.

Similarly, differences in socioeconomic status have been little studied, although families with greater economic resources and higher levels of education are generally expected to function better because they have the potential to understand the child's problem more readily and to buy helpful services more easily. In research on parenting in general, more educated families are typically found to provide more optimal parenting in certain ways; for example, explaining ideas to children more fully, exposing children to more aspects of culture, and encouraging reading. However, in the case of developmental disabilities, the opposite is possible, too: A developmentally disabled child may be seen as more markedly deficient and therefore may bring more shame to educated or wealthier parents, who may be less likely to accept a disabled child for who he or she is, rather than what they may have wanted him or her to be. If all the children in a family go to college except the developmentally disabled child, he or she may be seen as more different than in a family where one out of four children goes to college, two go to a trade school, and one just gets a job right out of high school. A mildly mentally retarded brother who is a night janitor may be seen as less deviant by an older sister who works as a salesclerk than by an older sister who works as an attorney. However, there has been no specific research to answer questions about family socioeconomic status and adjustment to having a handicapped child. We really don't know if parental adult-role expectations for their children cast a shadow on how positively or negatively the handicapped and the nonhandicapped siblings come to see their ability to feel personally successful.

A number of studies of families with children with a variety of handicaps have shown that the mother's mental health status is important to how well everyone else in the family adjusts to having a developmentally disabled brother or sister. If the mother has a psychiatric disorder like chronic depression, or an anxiety disorder, her ability to handle having a developmentally disabled child is decreased. In some cases, depression or an anxiety disorder may have been triggered by the stress of coping with the disabled child's extra needs. In other cases, a mother's psychiatric problems may have been a preexisting condition that has been made worse by the additional stress brought on by the disabled child. A substantial body of research shows that, whenever a mother has a psychiatric disorder, she is generally less available emotionally to her children, and that a substantial subgroup of such children make negative adjustments to their mother's unavailability. Siblings who do function well, even with an emotionally unavailable mother, probably learn a lot about coping by either emulating successful parental coping in their other parent or relying on emotional support from those outside the immediate family (like aunts, uncles, or grandparents), or because they simply have resilient personalities.

A parent who is emotionally confused or withdrawn is unlikely to be a good model or a good teacher for nonhandicapped siblings, who need guidance in responding to the difficulties caused by the handicapped sibling. For this reason, it is important that the mothers of developmentally disabled children seek psychotherapy for their own emotional distress, as the development of better coping will probably help not only them, but also their handicapped child and their other children.

Studies that have compared single- and two-parent families have shown that intact families tend to cope with a disabled child better than estranged families or single-parent families. No research has been done specifically on disabled children raised in extended families. It is known, however, that good social support—of which an extended family may be part—does promote better adaptation to the additional demands created by a handicapped child. Just as in the case with larger family sizes, the more people (children or adults) there are to share in the care of the disabled child, the less stressed everyone, particularly the mother, will be. Most studies have, in fact, focused on the role of mothers or on the strength of the family or marital relationships. Little research has focused specifically on the fathers of developmentally disabled children. In our clinical experience, however, a number of families seem to cope by "assigning" the handicapped child to the father, while the children who are not developmentally disabled appear to be "assigned" to the mother. That is, the father seems to be primarily responsible for taking the handicapped child to appointments, dealing with the child's school, and arranging special activities. In such families, the mothers, on the other hand, tend to carry out similar duties for the nonhandicapped children.

Another (less well-studied) family-functioning factor that predicts how well siblings will adjust is the degree of expressed emotion permitted. In families where expressing emotion in general—and expressing feelings about the developmentally disabled sibling in particular—is allowed, the children seem more protected from chronic stress responses like school failure or psychiatric disorders of their own. *Expressed emotion* is a jargony term used in stress research; it does not necessarily imply shouting and screaming about how angry one feels because of the handicapped child. *Expressed emotion* more often has positive connotations, as in the use of straightforward statements of feelings, or in the use of humor to ease the tension caused by the disabled child's inappropriate behavior.

Sibling Self-Reports

What have siblings themselves had to say about how they feel about having grown up with a handicapped brother or sister? How does what they say correlate with how they really feel and behave? One research concern is that preadolescent children have been heavily socialized by their parents in how to think and feel about their handicapped sibling. Most have certainly got the message not to say anything bad about their brother or sister to a stranger—even a nice stranger like a researcher asking the child to talk about the brother or sister. In fact, being asked direct questions may intensify the expression of attitudes about the brother or sister that the child has been trained to feel are right. Probably for this reason, researchers who have interviewed preadolescent children and researchers who have directly observed these children's interactions with their handicapped siblings have come up with somewhat different findings: Interviews tend to paint a picture of a minimum of distress about a sibling's disability. Direct observations tend to reveal more frustrations. There is some evidence that negative thoughts and feelings become "compartmentalized" and cut off from the rest of the child's thoughts and feelings at an early age. In one study that asked young children to describe their handicapped siblings, the investigators noted that the subjects often omitted the fact that a sibling had Down's syndrome or went to a special school. When researchers have examined the self-esteem or self-concept of the siblings of developmentally disabled children, no marked differences have appeared. However, self-concept and self-esteem are almost always measured by asking children to answer a standard series of questions describing themselves. In the process of giving answers, children may monitor their own behavior and express what they have learned is the "right" way to feel about life, and not what they truly feel. Therefore, especially in studies where self-report and observations do not correspond, it is unclear what was measured; true self-esteem or an idealized sense of self. Interestingly, although parents may socialize their children to feel that having negative feelings about their handicapped sibling or having negative feelings about their own lives because of their handicapped sibling is bad or wrong, one study reported that mothers saw their nonhandicapped sons as more aggressive and more depressed, and their nonhandicapped daughters as more depressed, than comparison mothers in families with no handicapped sibling. So even though parents may try to teach nonhandicapped children to compartmentalize their negative feelings, the parents may also be able to tell that such attempts have not been wholly successful.

There is still considerable controversy about the seemingly contradictory research in which the mothers seem more likely to see their children as depressed than the children themselves do. Some researchers feel that the siblings are depressed but are very good at hiding their feelings, and other researchers feel that the children are OK and that the higher levels of depression reported by their mothers are a projection of the mothers' own depressed feelings. Both or neither may be true, and clearly this is another area that needs more careful study. On an individual level, it is likely that, in some families, the mothers do see their own feelings of depression in their children. It is also likely that in some families, the children unconsciously work hard to defend themselves against their own feelings of depression; whereas in other families, the children who say they feel fine really do feel fine.

Severity of the Sibling's Handicap

Some researchers have looked at the question of how the severity of a child's mental retardation affects family coping. In these studies, the severity of the handicapped sibling's behavioral problems seemed more predictive of distress in family members than the level of mental retardation, *per se.* That is to say, some very severely retarded children are relatively pleasant and agreeable to care for, and other children who are actually not as mentally retarded may have behavioral difficulties associated with their particular handicap that make it especially hard for family members to have pleasurable interactions with them. There are some symptoms that are likely to be more difficult than others for non-handicapped brothers and sisters to adjust to:

1. Developmentally disabled children who are hyperactive tend to violate the "space" of brothers and sisters. Many parents tell stories, for example, of how a little sister has been sitting at the kitchen table coloring a picture for half an hour, only to have a big brother rush by and "accidentally" spill Coke all over it. (At that point, Mom's saying, "It was an accident, he didn't mean it" may be of little consolation.) Hyperactive children also tend to have difficulty waiting turns patiently (like not being first when ice-

cream cones get scooped), or giving their brothers and sisters equal time (like giving up the Nintendo after fifteen minutes), or not touching interesting things (like their brother's fragile model plane). In each of these cases, a negative outcome may generate rage or frustration at the handicapped sibling, which may or may not be expressed and may or may not earn a reprimand if it is expressed.

2. Another difficult symptom is self-centeredness. In one form it's the egocentricity of a two-year-old, although it may be less tolerable in a ten-year-old with a mental age of two. It's one thing for siblings to put up with the "terrible twos" for a year; it's another thing for them to put up with this behavior for eight years. In its most extreme form, self-centeredness is shown in the extreme aloofness and lack of care about or awareness of others found in autistic children. Many autistic children have little or no awareness that others have needs and desires in the same way that they do. For example, if the tub water is running, the autistic four-year-old may want to get in even if it's his eight-year-old sister's bath. If the autistic child has arranged books on a coffee table a certain way and his brother moves one of them (say, the book he needs to do his math homework), the autistic brother may scream, tantrum, and attempt to grab the book back and replace it to restore the order he has created. Autistic and other very egocentric mentally retarded children may also disturb siblings with their marked lack of empathy. For example, if a five-year-old sister falls off her two-wheel bike as she's learning to ride it, her autistic ten-year-old brother may laugh because the position she fell in looks funny to him.

3. Another area of handicap symptoms that presents conflicts for siblings is developmentally appropriate behavior. Parents may feel that the handicapped sibling really cannot be expected to eat with a fork, sit through dinner, stay in her or his bed after the lights are out, or help put away the toys in the family room. The non-handicapped siblings may resent this decision, either because they feel that their handicapped brother or sister *could* do the activity if their parents *made* her or him do it (in the same way the parents

make *them* do it), or simply that the rules are not being applied consistently.

4. One difficulty in understanding how the severity of a sibling's disability negatively affects the nonhandicapped siblings has to do with how the parents interpret "goodness" and "badness" in their children. One study of autistic children and their siblings found that the mothers who reported the most severe behavior problems in their autistic children also reported having the best behaved nonhandicapped children. It is hard to know whether the contrast between the two children caused these mothers to see them in sharper relief, or whether pressure to behave better actually grows stronger (and one actually does behave better) as one's sibling causes more problems. Possibly, both are true.

Moving from Research to Individual Cases

Research is a way of showing general trends and quantifying what is sometimes or often true in most cases. All the factors that have just been discussed interact in complex ways. Each family is different, although the principles extracted from research generally apply. Unfortunately, there has not been nearly enough research for us to begin to identify what to do about the problems encountered by the nonhandicapped siblings who are most at risk. In the two chapters that follow, the results of our clinical experience are added to this discussion of the research findings to provide further insight into the varied processes that may influence the development and difficulties encountered by the siblings of developmentally disabled children.

Chapter 3

A Family's Adjustment to a Developmentally Disabled Child

Nobody asks to be the parent of a handicapped child. No one plans for it. When it happens, it is never really expected. Everyone has anxieties and fears about whether a new baby will be "normal." Everyone hopes so. Everyone believes so. But when events don't turn out according to hopes and expectations, everyone in the family begins to change and adapt.

Many factors influence how a family *does* adapt to the added demands of having a handicapped child. This chapter enumerates those factors: We give examples of how families meet challenges, identify the stressors that make a family's ability to function grow worse, and also identify protective factors that help families cope.

If you are the sibling of a handicapped person and you are reading this chapter, it may give you some insight into the importance of what was going on in your family before your sibling arrived, and how those things may have made a difference in your family's functioning later on. If you are the parent of a handicapped child or adult, we hope this section will help you identify some of the confusing, hurtful, or frustrating things that have happened to you in the past, or that you still feel enmeshed in now. For the professional caregiver to the disabled or other health professional working with families with disabled children, this chapter is intended to assist in identifying the relative strengths and weaknesses of the families you treat, and in identifying areas where helpful interventions may be introduced.

The Relationship between the Parents

Every couple and every family can be described in terms of their strengths and weaknesses. As a family grows and changes, there are natural points at which the family functions better and at which the family functions worse. These points are influenced by many things related to how much in control of circumstances the family members feel themselves to be. Does the father feel that he is earning as good a living as he should be able to? How much work pressure is he experiencing? Is mother comfortable with the amount and type of work that she finds herself doing? Do the couple feel that they are living in a house or an apartment that will allow them to start a family or to have another child? What kind of social supports for their lifestyle do the couple have from relatives and friends? Does the extended family "approve" of the couple's relationship? Are the couple at a stage of life when friends and relatives are having children, too? How well do the couple get along?

All these questions are relevant considerations for any couple who contemplate having a baby. When the baby comes along and has a disability, the peaks and valleys of the social environment in which the couple find themselves are cast into high relief. Therefore, it is important to focus on all that surrounds the family and how it modifies the family's ability to do well in the task of raising a handicapped child.

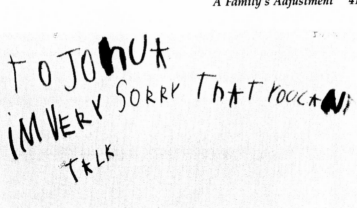

Figure 3.1 Naomi, Joshua's five-year-old sister, has summarized her brother's developmental difficulties according to the feature most noticeable to her—his lack of speech. At the time this drawing was made, Josh not only did not speak, but was diagnosed autistic as well. Her apology of "I'm sorry" reflects Naomi's sadness about her brother, as well as the latency-age child's rule-oriented thinking—that saying one is sorry is supposed to make right something that has gone wrong. In this case, the drawing may be Naomi's wish that saying "sorry" could give her the power to make Josh's problems all better.

Families with the best functioning before the birth or identification of a disabled child usually do better than families that did poorly before the added stress of a child with special needs. For example, one couple we have seen in our clinic had four children in six years. The first was deaf, the third was severely mentally retarded, and the fourth pregnancy was discovered when the mother went to have her tubes tied when the third child was five months old. This family had been coping poorly with having one disabled child even before the pregnancy with the fourth (and the disability of the third) was discovered. By the time the third child's mental retardation was discovered, the family was on the verge of collapse, and the mother had given the father an ultimatum: The third child had to be put up for adoption or she would leave and take the other three children with her. With the close spacing of so many children and the deafness in the first child, having the third child diagnosed with mental retardation was the straw that broke the camel's back.

Finding yourself the parent of a handicapped child hardly makes your life easier. However, for many families, the added stress not only magnifies the existing problems but creates whole new areas of conflict. It is helpful to examine what goes wrong with some families. It is also helpful to examine how creative some families are in adapting as well as possible.

Factors That Affect How Well Parents Raise Children Together

Marital Quality

A mental health professional who sits and talks to a couple about their disabled child develops a rather strong sense of how well the couple know one another and how well they get along: The couples who get along best seem to understand each other's strengths and weaknesses well. They are comfortable in verbalizing what their spouse can do best for their child as well as what they see as the difficulties the spouse is having. Careful words are used to convey what they understand about one another's feelings and opinions. A mother, glancing at her husband, may say, "I know that my husband and I have discussed a hundred times the time Billy had the 105-degree fever, and we still don't agree about what we should have done. I'll tell you what I think, and then I'd like him to tell you what he thinks." Often, there is a sense that such parents have discussed and scripted much of the dialogue before a doctor's appointment, so that neither spouse will inadvertently throw any surprise punches during the interview. Such couples are functioning well in protecting the mutually supportive resources of their relationship and generally have a better prognosis for positive coping.

However, not all couples who know each other well get along well. Some couples who know each other well use their knowledge to irritate and antagonize one another. For example, an unsupportive wife may say, "Well, I guess the reason my autistic son doesn't make any eye contact is because his father never makes any eye contact. Even my husband's mother used to nag him about it when he was a kid." When such a comment is made, the husband-father usually shifts uncomfortably in his seat and makes a momentary extra effort to make eye contact with the doctor. These kinds of parents take no solace from one another, and they are no joy for anyone else to be around. Sometimes, a minimal form of coping that is established by such couples is a ritualized style of fighting about the child. Generally, the older the disabled child is, the more ritualized are the interactions between the parents when discussing the child, and the more fixed each is in his or her own beliefs. For example, one parent may believe that the couple's retarded nonverbal sixteen-year-old son fully understands a television program that the rest of the family watches, while the other parent insists their son just likes to laugh when he hears the laugh track and has no idea of the show's plot. Often, such parents can predict verbatim what the other parent is going to say and then proceed to point out what each believes is fallacious about the other's statements. Such parents are really mired in hopelessness, and this hopelessness must be addressed before one can focus on the critical nature of their interchanges (which is an expression of the parents' pain). The day-to-day exhaustion of coping with their child's special needs leaves many couples little time or desire to directly address the conflicts that underlie the different understanding each has of the disabled child. Instead of their verbally discussing, adding to, and revising their ideas about the child, the views of each become fixed and become the repository of the most negative feelings each has involving the disabled child. Such couples are essentially withdrawn from new ideas and cannot take to heart the help or recommendations offered by anyone. Even if such parents are surrounded by potential sources of social support, they may find it difficult to use such resources.

Clinically, the preexisting stability of the parental relationship is a big factor in how well parents can work together in raising a disabled child. On the most basic level, *stability* refers to how long the couple have been together and how long they have been married. Other factors in the stability of a couple's relationship have to do with how culturally and religiously committed to their marriage they are, how supportive and involved their extended families are, and how well defined their views are of the roles of "mother" and "father." The couples that seem to cope best are those that have already been married for some time before the birth of their handicapped child. To a clinician who takes numerous pregnancy histories, it soon becomes clear that a fairly significant number of American marriages take place shortly after the conception of the first child. Usually, these couples already have some sort of steady relationship and are old enough so that having a baby is not an unreasonable thing to do together. However, in such histories, there is usually some implication about which one of the couple was "really" responsible for the pregnancy. If the child from the unplanned pregnancy turns out to be disabled, the other member of the couple may consciously or unconsciously assign the other parent the role of being the "more responsible parent" for that child. Subsequently, if the "more responsible parent" does not live up to his or her obligations, the other parent feels all the more wronged by the difficulties imposed by the presence of the child.

An issue closely related to who is "the more responsible parent" is where the disabled child fits into the family-planning pattern. Some children are simply unwanted but "had" anyway.

In other cases, the pregnancy was not explicitly planned (or not explicitly avoided), and when it occurs, the child is desired. A final group of children are those who are both wanted and planned. How well the family copes is often related to which of these groups a child falls into. Most families readily accept their responsibility for children who fall into the "wanted and planned" and the "wanted, but unplanned" categories.

The Unwanted Disabled Child

Children who are not planned but are simply "had" because the mother or father could not make a decision or agree to terminate the pregnancy often seem, clinically, the least accepted by their parents after the handicap is diagnosed. Basically, these children were unwanted by one or both parents to begin with, and the extra challenges presented by a developmental disability are not likely to make these children more acceptable. Interestingly, when the parents of such children stay together, the birth of the handicapped child is often followed by the birth of another child whom both parents plan and want, as if in hope of starting fresh and clearing away all the ambivalent feelings that both have toward the disabled child. Although the possibility has not been explicitly studied, these "makeup" babies may receive more attentive parenting than latter-born children who have followed a very wanted child who has turned out to be disabled.

When a pregnancy is unplanned, one or both parents may feel strongly that an abortion is not a possibility. Sometimes, a pregnancy is unwanted because the mother was on a binge of drinking or drug abuse in early pregnancy and fears that the fetus is already damaged (and it may be). Sometimes, denial of the severity of a substance abuse problem takes the form of maintaining the pregnancy, even though the child is not really wanted. If this attitude continues throughout the pregnancy, the child is usually given up at birth or shortly after the child's disabling condition is identified (if the child isn't involuntarily removed anyway because of continued substance abuse). Close family members may encourage maintaining the pregnancy even though neither parent really wants a child. Sometimes, it is these family members who end up parenting the child. We have followed a number of children who are being raised by their grandmothers as the mothers continue to lead lives devoid of any sense of stability or responsibility. (Often, such mothers, particularly poly-substance-abusing mothers, produce one unplanned, unwanted handicapped child after another; the result may be two or three brothers or sisters with varying degrees of disability, with the less handicapped ones partly standing in as parents for the more handicapped ones.) In one family we tried to help, a seven-year-old sister, who herself had delayed language, was quite serious and maternal as the primary caregiver for her three-year-old moderately retarded, hyperactive brother and a ten-month-old brother, with whom she spent unaccompanied evenings in a single-room-occupancy hotel room while her mother partied and did drugs. Although this little girl's efforts were admirable, they certainly should have been uncalled for, and the toll they took on her was recorded in the violent play she acted out with a mommy doll and a number of "boyfriend" dolls. Of course, this degree of psychopathology and distress is unusual; most siblings do get more parental support. However, siblings do have more of a gap to fill if they sense that the parent is unusually withdrawn from the handicapped sibling because that sibling is unwanted.

Two other groups have a high risk of producing unwanted developmentally disabled children, and they are worth mentioning at this point: (1) women who are developmentally disabled themselves and (2) severely mentally ill women. Sometimes, these children are not so much unwanted as they are conceived by women who are too fuzzy to use even rudimentary birth control. Many times, these women don't realize they are pregnant until it is too late to obtain an abortion. We have evaluated a number of cases of retarded children born to retarded mothers in which both mother and child were cared for by the maternal grandparents. One worries whether, in these cases, the grandparents may feel obligated to raise the grandchild as well—as if they still need to pay for whatever sin brought them their retarded daughter. In our experience, the developmentally disabled adults who become parents tend to stay within the nexus of their families, so that, when they have children, the children are often supported by the extended family. Sometimes, the biological mother functions more as the disabled child's older sibling than as the mother—taking directions about child care from *her* mother, and caring for the baby mainly to earn the grandmother's approval.

A similar problem of unwanted developmentally disabled children is presented by the pregnancies of severely mentally ill mothers. The severely mentally ill are much more often estranged from their families, and when they have children, there is no similar family support system. One schizophrenic couple known to our clinic has had two children together (eleven months apart). In both cases, the couple's parental rights were terminated at birth by child protective services because the mother was so badly decompensated that she was actively hallucinating during labor. Both of these children—Melissa, now age six, and Ira, now age five—were adopted at birth by single women who subsequently became friends because of their children's birth relationship. Melissa can now be described as a little language-delayed; and Ira is autistic. The misfortune is that both children are developmentally disabled, but the wonderful thing is how the adoptive parents, in the absence of other family support, have discovered a unique support system in one another. Although developmentally disabled children such as these are not strictly "unwanted" by their birth parents, they are wanted for unrealistic reasons by disabled parents who have no idea of how to care for a special child, and who have no support system for either themselves or their children. When at least one nonhandicapped child is born to such parents and the parents *do* manage to keep their children, the nonhandicapped child often becomes a caregiver not only for the disabled siblings but for the parents as well.

There is only so much little children can do to help one another when their parents keep producing children because they lack the judgment to know that they will be unable to care for them adequately. In another case, concerning three developmentally delayed girls (six, four, and two years old) who had two schizophrenic parents, the lack of social support for the family prevented the marginally functional father from understanding the breadth of the developmental problems of each of his girls (e.g., why they needed to go to special school); eventually, the courts took the children away, charging him with criminal child neglect and abuse, and he had another psychotic break when the verdict found him guilty on several counts. In this case, each of the three girls began to improve developmentally and psychologically, after having been removed from the parents.

Although some family members (or expectant parents) may briefly harbor the romantic notion that having to care for a disabled child will inspire a dysfunctional adult to "straighten up and fly right," or to get clean and sober, or to take his or her antipsychotic medication regularly, it seldom happens. Normal siblings caught up in the dynamics of such a family get a double dose of mistreatment—from inadequate parents and from the extra demands of caring for difficult siblings.

The Unplanned but Desired Child

Many parents report pregnancies as unplanned but desired. Some families can't quite make the decision to "try," and others don't like the idea of having sex on a schedule. Families that find themselves with a disabled child to care for generally cope adequately if the child was desired, even if the timing of the pregnancy was not planned down to the month or year. Sometimes, though, such pregnancies occur when one or more family circumstances are not as optimal as they might have been in a year or two. In our clinical experience, we have seen families in which the penultimate stressor in the birth of a disabled child has been the parents' not yet having finished school or having to defer a plan to move to a larger home, or the birth of the disabled child's coming when the family are living temporarily away from extended family, when a grandparent has just died, or when the father has been in the military and away on a tour of duty when the baby was born. Most families may not see such circumstances as major enough stressors to feel that the pregnancy is ill advised, but coupled with the birth of a child who requires special attention, such minor stressors can make a serious impact. When a child with a disability is born into such circumstances, it is likely that more responsibility will fall to the older siblings, and maladaptive patterns of family functioning are then in place by the time subsequently born children arrive.

The Planned Child with a Disability

For families who have carefully planned the arrival of their baby, having a baby who turns out to have special needs may be a double-edged sword. Such families have usually considered all of the social supports available to their family and have decided that the time is right, and that stressors are at a minimum, manageable, or at least acknowledged in light of how they will be handled with a new baby in the family. Often, the families that plan children in this way have better family and economic resources anyway. What may make it more difficult for such families to cope with accepting a disabled child is that many precautions have typically been taken to prevent anything's going wrong. The women get in shape before their pregnancies, quit smoking, stop drinking even a glass of wine while trying to get pregnant; and take not even an aspirin or an antihistamine. Once the pregnancy is confirmed, the most careful prenatal care regimen is followed, and any comments by the obstetrician are dissected for all their possible implications. Therefore, when the child's disability is diagnosed, either at birth or later, the parents tend to make a terribly guilt-ridden review of what they could have done differently that might have prevented this outcome. If either parent finds any reason to believe that something was nonoptimal about the pregnancy or the delivery, and that he or she somehow failed to act, this belief may set up a dynamic of helplessness with respect to dealing with other circumstances that involve the child's developmental status in the future, especially medical concerns. This same sort of guilt is found in women with "desired but unplanned pregnancies," but at least any events that transpired before the pregnancy was diagnosed can be seen (at least on a conscious level) as a risk that was known and acknowledged at the time. So, for instance, a mother who blames herself for her child's retardation (for example, by failing to control her blood sugar sufficiently well through diet during pregnancy) may fail to follow through on having the child's blood levels monitored for anticonvulsant medications to best control his seizure disorder. Families that have planned their children very carefully often express a greater sense of the "unfairness" of having had a developmentally disabled child than families that live their lives with less planning.

Other Parenting Stressors

Single Parents

Without doubt, the most difficult situation to cope with is parenting a disabled child as a single parent. It is probably in these situations that the nonhandicapped siblings are most stressed. A spouse is usually the most available form of social support, and without one, the single parent has the full-time primary responsibility for the special-needs child. These single mothers (we have seen very few primary caregivers of children with special needs who are fathers) are faced with the myriad of problems faced by all single parents, multiplied by the extra time and other costs of having a handicapped child. Again, as social support decreases, parental dependence on nonhandicapped siblings tends to increase.

Single parents go it alone through either choice or necessity. The first time a clinician sees a little three-year-old sibling take her retarded five-year-old brother firmly by the hand as they are about to cross a busy street, the idea of how much the life of the three-year-old is being affected by having a handicapped brother becomes clear. The risk for these children of becoming parentified is really substantial, whether they are younger or older than their disabled sibling. Typically, the nonhandicapped sibling is assigned specific roles in caring for his or her disabled sibling, usually including things like physically guarding the disabled sibling's movements so he or she doesn't do anything dangerous. Even though the nonhandicapped siblings may be of an age where they themselves should be watched for such behavior, they become the "keeper" instead of the "kept." Amazingly, most siblings rise to these occasions well, and I've seen numerous pieces of chalk, Leggos, and Fisher-Price Peg People being removed from the mouths of retarded children by five-, six-, and seven-year-old brothers and sisters. When policing tasks like these go well, the siblings feel good about doing their job, and they have certainly found a way to earn appreciation from their overwhelmed mother. The opposite is true when the mission fails, and the disabled child begins to gag or breaks something, and the little seven-year-old feels like an abject failure.

In some of the best situations, a single-parent mother with a handicapped child receives substantial support from her family. We've had many single mothers come to my clinic with their mothers (i.e., the patient's maternal grandmother). In some ways, grandmothers may be ideal supports because they tend to know more about how children develop, and they often seem to accept a handicapped child more easily, despite his limitations, than the parent does. In general, grandparents seem less often unable to take action because of denial of a child's disability and are more often ready to undertake a pragmatic approach to the child's treatment. It is hard to say why. Maybe older people come from a generation in which less educated people were more common, and the idea that a "handicapped" child who will never graduate from high school or learn to read and write seems less horrible than to a generation of parents who believe that anyone who does not read, write, and graduate from high school is some sort of failure.

Younger single mothers in particular seem willing to accept their mothers as authorities and therefore welcome their mothers' taking instrumental roles in making decisions about the handicapped child's special needs.

Obviously, one factor in how single mothers cope is the degree, if any, of involvement of the child's father. Joint custody may be very helpful, as it gives respite to both parents. Unfortunately, many mentally retarded children do best in an environment with a high degree of unvarying structure. Some parents try to create this structure by leaving the child at one house and moving themselves every week or two. Even in this type of arrangement, it is almost impossible for the two parents to be consistent in terms of behavior they expect or won't accept. Sometimes, therefore, the necessary consistency and continuity must be supplied by a sibling, especially an older sibling. The Stark family is an example. Amid a hostile, and seemingly never-ending child-custody dispute, Angela, age eight, and her autistic brother, Jake, age five, go back and forth from their mother Linda's laissez-faire 1960s-style Berkeley home to the more highly organized home of their remarried attorney father. As Jake is autistic, if certain things are not just so, he may become quite difficult indeed, so it falls on Angela to make sure that Jake's cowboy pajamas go with him from house to house. If they don't, all hell breaks loose—and Angela feels responsible. Angela also must take the role of interpreter of all the oblique and tangential things that Jake has to say, because she has a more continuous view of his experience than anyone else, and Jake cannot speak with other people's perspective in mind.

Very occasionally, custody disputes over handicapped children work in the reverse of usual custody disputes: On more than one occasion, I've been involved in cases in which the parents are not fighting over who *will* have the child, but over who *won't* have the child. Sometimes, these disputes are resolved with an agreement that, in order to get the nonhandicapped siblings, the litigating parent must also agree to accept the handicapped one. Although one can see the "justice" in this resolution, it can also be seen as an opportunity lost that could otherwise allow the nonhandicapped siblings at least some time in a family with one of their parents and without the responsibilities and limitations imposed by their handicapped sibling.

Parental Age and Approaches to Child Rearing

Among the families we see, there is a broad range—from younger couples in their mid-twenties to older couples in their mid-forties—all of whom are trying to understand and accept the diagnosis of a cognitive disability in their child. Although there are many individual differences, the younger couples often seem able to cope somewhat better than the older couples. There may be several reasons: The younger parents just have more physical energy. Their lifestyle patterns are not so fixed. They are young enough to have more children, even to wait a number of years until they do so. Perhaps younger couples have not had so many years to develop idealized fantasies of what family life should be like and instead take things more as they come.

On the other hand, for the older couples, the inevitability of deciding to have a child is usually less. Perhaps the most poignant example I can think of is an upper-class South American couple: The wife was in her early forties, and the husband was in his early fifties. He had grown children in their early thirties. She had never had a child, and they had adopted a baby from an orphanage in their country of origin. By age three, it was clear that the child was severely mentally retarded. The marriage was failing. She had begged for a child and now was crushed because she had never envisioned motherhood as so difficult and was hating herself as a mother. We suggested that the couple return the child to the orphanage and try to resume the positive aspects of their marriage. (This is not the course we would have recommended had this been a natural child.) The father was tearful but tried to remain stoic. The mother cried. A few months later, we heard through a member of a support group the couple had attended that the child *had* gone back, and that, for them, it had been the right decision.

For other older couples, the child born with a developmental problem may have been a "surprise," arriving after a number of years of infertility or the presumed onset of menopause. The risk of a number of mental retardation syndromes, the most common of which is Down's syndrome, increases with maternal age. For example, the risk of Down's syndrome increases to 1 in 88 births by age forty-five. Nevertheless, and even though many older couples now go through genetic counseling and amniocentesis, most still seem as shocked as younger couples when they find they have a child with a genetic disorder that has a higher prevalence in older mothers. No couple think it could happen to them. Surprisingly, although genetic counselors routinely explain that amniocentesis rules out only disorders with known genetic etiologies, and that there are still no known gene markers for the majority of congenital anomalies and mental retardation syndromes, most parents feel protected from having a disabled child once the amniocentesis comes back negative. In our clinic, we have interviewed scores of parents who have expressed shock that their child could be cognitively handicapped when the amniocentesis was normal. Although some of these parents may not have fully appreciated the disclaimers that genetic counselors present, others seem to rely on "science" to support a denial that having a child at an older age presents some real risks. In any case, the anger caused by the child's disability is sometimes displaced onto the geneticists, who parents feel misled them. Ultimately, as in other circumstances where the parents feel let down by a potential support system (in this case, doctors), feelings of helplessness and hopelessness about the child's situation may follow. Once parents do understand that doctors cannot give a written prenatal guarantee against disabilities, and once one disabled child has already been born, the level of trepidation with which subsequent pregnancies is undertaken is usually fairly high. So, another pressure on latter-born siblings can be to continually achieve, in order to constantly reassure their parents that they have no undetected disability. We discuss this subject more in Chapter 9.

In other cases, the child with a disability may be a product of a later second marriage for one or both of the parents, and there are already much older children on the mother's and/or the father's side. There seems to be more ambivalence about having children among those older couples who have already had children, and the negative side of the ambivalence sometimes seems to be vindicated when the child turns out to have a disability.

The pattern of "ambivalence turned to anger" may occur less often in older couples who have simply delayed child rearing for a number of years, because the couple either married late or spent many years establishing their careers before having children. Such couples often seem to feel melancholy about their child's disability but nonetheless cope fairly well. One couple we follow unexpectedly had their only child, Turner, after years of infertility, when the mother was in her early forties, and the father in his late fifties. For the first fifteen years, they saw their profoundly retarded son as a rather inevitable outcome of a conception that wasn't meant to be. Only at age fifty-five did Turner's mother shift her exclusive attention from training her son, interestingly, toward becoming certified as a nursery school teacher (perhaps as a last chance to experience normal child rearing). In families such as Turner's, one wonders whether the parents would have directed such exclusive efforts toward the child's development if there had been siblings with competing needs.

Parental Denial and Its Relation to Social Support

Parental denial of a child's disability plays a major role in how the rest of the family members are affected by the child's presence. Some aspects of parental denial feed into the marital strain that may arise from parenting a developmentally disabled child and are discussed later in the context of the parents' relationship. Of relevance here, parental denial may be due to a lack of social support, or to support from sources that are perceived as hostile. As has already been illustrated, parental denial may sometimes be fed by a lack of awareness of how children are supposed to develop. For parents of only children (or of a firstborn before the birth of a sibling), denial of developmental problems may be increased by a lack of information or any basis for comparison. It is in these situations, where the parents have little prior knowledge of child development, that relatives and friends often feel most justified in trying to point out the developmental delays that they feel are present in the child. Depending on the quality of the preexisting relationship between the parents and the friend or relative giving advice, the parents may be helped to understand the child's problems or may be driven deeper into denial.

An example is the case of Kathleen, whose four-and-a-half-year-old son, Eric, was severely language-delayed and mute. Kathleen came from a high-achieving family; her parents were wealthy, her two siblings were physicians, and she herself was well educated but was an unemployed agoraphobic alcoholic, married to an unsuccessful businessman who was almost her parents' age. Kathleen could at least feel superior to her psychiatrist sister because she was married and had Eric. So when Eric was two and a half, and Kathleen's psychiatrist sister began to point out Eric's developmental problems, Kathleen took these comments as jealous, competitive hostility (which it may have been) and ignored the truthful component of her sister's observations for two years.

On the other hand, family support can work positively to break through a couple's denial about their child's disability. Another family we follow, the Johns, have three children, eight-year-old Robert and twin four-year-olds, David and Clara. David is autistic but was not diagnosed until age four because his mother, Martha, has a history of chronic and debilitating depressions, which were severely exacerbated by the recent diagnosis of David. In the course of evaluating and planning for David, we received letters explaining Martha's own psychiatric status, concerns about David's development, and general family concern about how the Johns could learn to cope better, as well as great willingness to help, from aunts on both sides of the family, including one who flew out from New York to help organize the family. Eventually, the maternal grandparents took David to live with them for a time in the Midwest, because of fear that Martha would have to be hospitalized if not separated from the child by other means. With David out of the home, Martha evened out a little, got treatment for herself, and began some acceptance of David's condition. Clearly, without family support in getting to and accepting David's diagnosis, Martha's denial would have continued, David would have remained untreated, and Robert and Clara would have continued to be neglected as Martha would have spent increasing amounts of time isolating herself from the realities of her children's needs.

Many relatives have a potential for misunderstanding the nature of a child's developmental disorder, and when family members get together, there may be a reluctance to discuss the child's problems explicitly. It is really up to the parents of the disabled child to take the initiative in establishing a dialogue that will help extended-family members feel that they really know what is going on with the disabled child. This approach is important because knowledge usually breeds empathy in relatives. If relatives feel that they can't be let in on information about a child who obviously has a developmental problem, they may feel less valued as confidants. It is important for parents to keep the channels of communication with relatives open so that unhandicapped siblings can have normality in this aspect of family life. Parents shouldn't want to end up resenting or feeling angry at friends and relatives who appear to not understand their situation. This attitude only serves to isolate a family further and can have a harmful effect on nondisabled siblings.

Extended-Family Social Support and the Nonhandicapped Siblings

It is bittersweet to accept advice and help from family and friends about a developmentally disabled child. Siblings of a handicapped child may feel like "charity cases" when taken on by an aunt's or uncle's family so that they can do something they can't do with their own mother and father because of a handicapped brother or sister. On the other hand, such occasions provide the opportunity to participate in special activities that might otherwise not come to pass. Some siblings have fantasies about belonging to that other family, to allow themselves to feel more normal, less stressed, and less responsible for their handicapped brother or sister. This is a normal feeling, and many children growing up fantasize about belonging to other families as a way of addressing their dissatisfactions with their parents.

Parental Problems in Confronting the Disabled Child's Diagnosis

Adaptation and Timing of the Diagnosis

A major factor in how a family copes with the diagnosis of a developmental disability in a child is when and how the disability is first diagnosed. Diagnoses of disabilities usually occur at one of three points in time: (1) prenatally as the result of amniocentesis or some other prenatal diagnostic test such as an alpha-fetal protein test (for spina bifida) or an ultrasound test; (2) perinatally, at the time of birth, when either obvious birth trauma occurs or an unusual physical appearance results in the diagnosis of a congenital syndrome; or (3) as the child matures, and it becomes apparent that her or his development is not the same as that of other children of the same age. Broadly, there are some differences in how families experience the stress of a disabled child depending on when the diagnosis is made and what responsibility the family assumes for the child's having the disability.

Prenatally Identified Disabilities

At present, it is technologically possible through amniocentesis or chorionic villus sampling to identify a number of birth defects responsible for genetic defects. The most common form of mental retardation with a known genetic marker, Down's syndrome, and fragile X syndrome can be tested prenatally. In addition, blood tests, such as that for excessively high levels of alpha-fetal protein, can reveal a baby who will be born with spina bifida, which causes physical defects of the spine and motor abilities, as well as mental retardation in many affected children. Some gene markers, such as for fragile X and Turner's syndrome in girls, are of variable penetrance; that is, some children born with the disorder may be only mildly affected with learning disabilities, and others have severe mental retardation. When there are positive findings on such a test, it is not possible to say whether a particular case will turn out to be a mild or a severe one.

Once prenatal testing is done and a result comes back positive, the parents face a severe dilemma: They must decide on action or no action. Most, though not all, couples who undertake prenatal testing do so with the implicit understanding that if the baby has a known defect, they will consider termination of the pregnancy. (A much smaller number of couples just want to "know" about their baby and are clear that, on religious or other moral grounds, they would never terminate a pregnancy no matter what the findings.) Couples are faced with an "easy" decision if the positive result involves a syndrome where the baby is seldom born alive or inevitably dies shortly after birth. The difficult decisions are those confronted by couples who know their baby will definitely be born with a mental retardation syndrome but have no way of knowing whether their baby will be mildly or severely affected. When the decision at this point is to maintain the pregnancy, the parents are more fully accepting responsibility for a handicapped child than in any other circumstance. In our clinical experience, these are usually either parents with strong religious principles or very naive, uneducated people using fantastic amounts of denial. After the child is born, the former group generally does relatively well, and the latter group generally does more poorly. Occasionally, I am consulted by families who have just found out that they are expecting a child with Down's syndrome or fragile X. Some professionals advise such people to visit infant stimulation programs to see what babies with Down's syndrome are like. I advise them to visit a group home for adults with Down's syndrome, too.

Once the decision is made to maintain a pregnancy when it is known that the new baby will be disabled, an incredible psychological Rubicon is crossed. Perhaps the reason that families with strong religious principles do relatively better after making such a decision is that the decision is mutual, the grounds for making the decision are clear, and a third party of sorts (such as their church) can be seen as the "real" decision maker, rather than one parent or the other. Conversely, in the other families that decide to have a disabled child in the hope or belief that the case will be as mild as possible, one parent (in my clinical experience, usually the father) leads the decision making. This decision irrevocably changes the balance of responsibility for the child, consciously or unconsciously, in the minds of both parents.

Perinatally Identified Disabilities

Most often, when a woman is younger than thirty-two to thirty-five years old, prenatal testing is not recommended unless there is a known family history of some heritable genetic disorder. Although a baby with a genetic or other congenital defect is less often born to such a young mother, it happens. Often, the baby's disorder is identified at the time of birth or before the baby goes home from the hospital. The high excitement of the birth is countervailed by the devastating news of the abnormal finding. The term *roller coaster* does not begin to convey the sensations of parents who go through this experience. If they comprehend it. Pediatricians and neonatologists are familiar with the scenario of pulling themselves together to tell parents that their baby almost died at birth; that there was no breathing at first; that the baby turned gray blue; that the baby was almost asphyxiated by aspirating meconium; or that there was injury to the skull by the forceps. The pediatrician may say something like, "This little guy is lucky to be here." Often the pediatrician is implying that the baby is likely to suffer permanent sequelae. Sometimes, the parents only hear the pediatrician's words to mean, "Now that's over, he's breathing fine, and so he's all right." For these parents, the child's disability may not become apparent until the child's development begins to seem different, and it is then that they go back over the pediatrician's words and realize what she or he was really saying.

A version of perinatally diagnosed developmental disabilities that is possibly most stressful on family functioning in general and on siblings in particular is when the affected sibling is born a fragile premature baby. These days, twenty-four- and even twenty-two-week premature babies survive, and not a small number have some degree of developmental disability later on. Premature babies that are born very early and/or very sick present some of the same problems as when a particular syndrome is diagnosed at birth: In both types of cases, it is hoped that this baby will have the best possible outcome for those with the same diagnosis or birth circumstances, but in both cases, the baby *is* seen as at risk, and very anxious, vigilant care usually follows once the baby is home. The birth of very little premature babies is probably even harder on nonhandicapped siblings in the first few months than when the affected sibling is an unexpected Down's syndrome baby. All older children are jealous, to some extent, of a new baby. This jealousy is much worse if the mother is at the hospital with the new baby constantly and is too worried or stressed to engage in the usual pleasurable activities with her older children, who react by feeling all the more abandoned. During the mother's pregnancy, the siblings will have developed fantasies about what it will be like to be the brother or sister of the new baby. If the baby does not come home from the hospital as planned, the sibling may feel that his or her fantasies are being ruined and, rather irrationally, may blame the baby. This type of egocentric thinking is especially predominant among children who are less than five or six years old. When the premature baby does come home, the research literature suggests that the parents continue to treat it in certain preferential ways, even when no firm signs of developmental abnormality exist. In such cases, even before the parents discover the child's disability, the child is already being treated as if he or she has one, and the demands of the siblings are being deferred.

Disabilities That Become Apparent as the Child Develops

In the majority of children with developmental disabilities of all sorts, the cause is described as *idiopathic*, a term meaning that there is no apparent known cause. Sometimes, risk factors are present, such as illness during pregnancy or problems during the delivery. However, many people make relatively little of these factors at the time because, on a case-by-case basis, it is always possible to point to children exposed to these same risk factors who develop perfectly normally. These sorts of risk factors include events like bleeding during the pregnancy, excessive weight gain or toxemia in the mother, and low Apgar scores at birth. These factors gain attention only after the child's development is suspect, and the parents soon dread having to repeat the litany of these risk factors each time an opinion is sought from another specialist.

The Effects of Pointing the Finger of Blame

As the risk factors are enumerated, the mettle of parental mutual support is tested, as it is possible for each risk factor to be accompanied by finger pointing by spouses—most of which has no empirical basis, but which definitely satisfies an emotional need to identify a cause and apportion blame. For example, a child identified as having fetal alcohol syndrome will be "blamed" on the mother (although she was probably drinking with the father). If the father has a mentally retarded first cousin, even if the first cousin is believed to be retarded because of a birth injury, the disabled child will be "blamed" on the father. There is a lot for a clinician to learn about the couple based on how irrational the blaming is, and on how fixed they seem in their beliefs about what "caused" the child's disorder. Some couples get fixated on this stage and can't begin to cope with raising the child until they realize that it doesn't help the child at all to "resolve" the blame issue. Until the couple can put the blame issue aside, they continue to be adversaries instead of a team working together to help the child.

When blame is not set aside, the adversarial relationship between the parents continues and tends to enhance the polarization of the spouses, especially with respect to the treatment of the disabled child. Usually, the opposition of the spouses is soon translated into a series of adversarial positions on how to help the disabled child: how to teach him, how to discipline him, what to expect him to be able and unable to do, and how efficacious or hindering the other spouse's efforts are in helping the child. Siblings may be recruited into one adversarial position or the other and, as a result, must cope with conflicting loyalties to their parents and a poor understanding of what they really can do to help their handicapped brother or sister. The reality is that, because we know so little about what causes the majority of developmental disorders, each parent will hold theories that, at least for the present, can't be substantiated or disproved by scientific findings.

The families that we see clinically, and that cope the best with the unresolved issues of etiology, are those that believe fervently in equal time for the opposing points of view. In interviews with such parents, they jump right in and preempt the doctor by saying, "I know my husband sees this differently, and I think it's important that you hear what he has to say, too." The key is that open discussion leads to a deferral of blame. In turn, having open discussions about the origin of the child's problems leads such couples to be able to depend on one another and to use one another as sounding boards for the issues that arise in parenting their developmentally disabled child. And as parental harmony concerning the disabled child increases, the siblings adapt better because mention of their disabled brother's or sister's problems by either parent does not mean that the stage is being set for parental conflict in which they may be pawns.

The Age of Recognition
and the Age of Diagnosis

A difficult time for families, and one during which the behavioral requirements for the nonhandicapped siblings with respect to the handicapped sibling are formed, is between the *age of recognition* and the *age of diagnosis*. The age of recognition is the time when parents begin to feel that something is wrong with their child. There are actually two ways of characterizing the age of recognition: First, there is the time when the parents began to talk to each other about their concerns about the child, or when a friend, relative, or doctor has brought up the subject. Second—and this occurs after the age of diagnosis—parents sometimes go back to an even earlier point when they had suspicions that something was wrong, but did not feel there was enough to be concerned about to express it to the spouse or to anyone else. For example, on a home video, an eighteen-month-old autistic girl, Jena, jumps and flaps her hands at water running out of a gutter. Her parents called it Jena's "rain dance." By the time she was four, they realized that Jena's "rain dance" was symptomatic of the stereotyped motor movements associated with some cases of autism and mental retardation. Sometimes, quite a period of time elapses between the age of recognition and the age of diagnosis, that is, when the child is actually first "labeled" with a disability or disorder. During this period, the parents may grow more anxious about whether there really is a problem, and about whether it seems to be something the child is showing signs of outgrowing, or whether there is evidence that the problem is getting worse. It is at this time that siblings can become a problem. It's not that the siblings are doing anything wrong; it's what they are doing right that highlights their sibling's increasingly obvious disabilities.

During a diagnostic evaluation for a developmental disorder, parents are inevitably asked whether little John or Jane's brothers or sisters have problems that are anything like what the parents fear is wrong with John or Jane. Quite often, the parents tell the examiner that, in fact, the brother or sister is exceptionally advanced or gifted. Occasionally, of course, this is true, but studies do not confirm higher IQs for most siblings of disabled children. What the parents often do is attribute some of the gap between their children to the nonhandicapped child's being unusually bright, rather than to the disabled child's being further behind than they realize. This perception kills two narcissistic birds with one stone and is a very natural, normal defensive response: The nonhandicapped child is perceived as brighter than he really is; the handicapped child is perceived as less disabled than he is.

Explaining Developmental Disability to Nonhandicapped Siblings

A watershed for many parents occurs when they realize that they must say something to their nonhandicapped children about what is wrong with their handicapped brother or sister. In some developmental disabilities where there are also obvious physical congenital anomalies, this is not an issue. The other siblings learn right away that something is wrong and subsequently attribute all other observations of unusual behavior to the disorder.

How can parents best communicate with their nondisabled children about the nature of the handicapped child's problems? The answer depends largely on the nonhandicapped children's age, and on how obvious the sibling's disability is, physically and behaviorally. Thinking about how children conceptualize physical illness at different developmental stages gives us some insight into how children are likely to be able to understand developmental disabilities as they grow.

Toddlers' Ability to Understand Developmental Disorders

By the second year of life, children just beginning to talk have a good set of templates of how people of different ages are supposed to look physically and of how people usually act. A child who is very dysmorphic or otherwise physically disabled will be a source of curiosity for a two-year-old who has not seen such a child before. One two-year-old, Paul, whom we observed seeing a severely retarded girl with bilateral hearing aids commented, "Girl—headphones." As the girl rocked rhythmically, stereotypically picking up and dropping a set of car keys, Paul commented further, "Girl—music." It was possible to tell from this two-year-old's close attention to the girl that he was not quite satisfied with his explanation, but he had come as close as he could, given the previous observations he had made. The situation is different for siblings who grow up with a disabled brother or sister. If they are younger, they are accustomed to the differences from the beginning. If they are older, they incorporate the differences much as their parents do (who, for example, sometimes lose the ability to see that their child with Down's syndrome looks dysmorphic).

In developmental disorders in which the sibling looks normal, the parents have a harder time deciding what to tell their nondisabled children. Usually, the parents put off this moment as long as possible, perhaps because "telling" adds another layer of reality and finality to the disabled child's status, or perhaps because they feel that the siblings will begin to stigmatize and reject their brother or sister if they find a "label" for what is wrong. Often, the nondisabled siblings question their parents, and the parents must begin to explain the handicapped child's disability.

Preschoolers' Ability to Understand Developmental Disorders

Recognition of the behavioral, as opposed to the physical traits of developmental disorders requires a higher level of cognition. Depending on their severity, behavioral differences will be noticeable to nonhandicapped siblings at different ages. Usually, the first thing siblings detect (often by age three or four) is that their disabled sibling doesn't talk. Children are aware that speech is a universal characteristic in children who are not infants and toddlers, and they start to ask why their brother or sister can't talk, usually by the time the disabled sibling is three. Parents sometimes hesitate to tell nonhandicapped siblings anything about what is wrong, either because they don't yet fully understand themselves, or because they fear stigmatizing one of their children in the eyes of the others.

The approach we recommend is to explain to the other children *something* about the disability. Denying that they are making accurate observations only diminishes their sense of open communication with their parents and denies them the freedom to express their concerns and anxieties about their disabled sibling. In talking to siblings about disability, parents can look on a diagnostic label as an empty box: Observations about the brother or sister that don't fit the template of typical behavior can be put in that box. A term like *disability* or *mentally retarded* or *handicapped* or *autistic* has no intrinsic meaning to a four-, five-, or six-year-old. Using the right words from the beginning is probably the best way for parents to proceed in teaching a young child *not* to stigmatize handicapped people.

Children under age four or five are extremely egocentric and tend to think that everything happens for them or because of them. If children are at this age when they realize a sibling has a disability, they may believe that the disability was caused by their own actions or thoughts. They may recall hitting or injuring their sibling without getting caught, and they may consciously or unconsciously blame at least some of the abnormality on that incident. They may be quite frightened by abnormal behavior and may not understand that abnormal behavior is not catching. For example, a three-year-old boy who often witnesses epileptic seizures may feel that they can happen to him, too. A four-year-old girl who is becoming very self-conscious of her behavior and appearance may be frightened by incontinence following a seizure and may believe that she will fall down and wet herself in nursery school sometime, too. It is important for parents to help their nondisabled children to understand that they will not develop the handicapped sibling's symptoms. Preschoolers who have learned that one can "catch" a cold by drinking from the same cup as someone who is sneezing and coughing may believe that they can "catch mental retardation" the same way. This may be the reason that a preschooler becomes very resistant to touching his disabled sibling or sharing toys. (It also may be normal three-year-old jealousy and self-centeredness.)

Sometimes, parents have inadvertently said something in another context that leads the nonhandicapped siblings to the wrong idea about the affected child's disability: A five-year-old was asked why she was avoiding her brother. She explained that her brother had caught autism when he was little from a bug, and that she was afraid that it might happen to her as well. Instead of explaining that autism is not caused by a bug, and trying to describe what it really is, it would be more appropriate to ease this child's fears in terms she can understand. The parent or doctor might explain that "The type of bug that can cause this illness can do it only before a baby is born. And once the bug is inside someone, it can't get out and go into someone else. So you are safe." This last statement is all the child really wants or needs to hear when she's five years old. Giving additional details would only complicate matters and not lay any fears to rest. Certainly, the explanation offered above is consistent with the truth, as some cases of autism seem to be caused by a viral illness in utero that results in a problem only under certain conditions; once inside the body, it can do no harm to others.

Preschoolers also may learn to understand disability through comparison: One mother described how her six-year-old, Jessica, had been playing at her friend Amanda's house: Amanda had a three-year-old brother, too—but Amanda's brother talked a blue streak, built with blocks, didn't have to wear a bib for drooling, and could drink from a cup. When Jessica came home, her comments showed her mother that she was beginning to realize that something was different about *her* brother. Until then, he had just been her baby brother, and she had thought that's how babies were supposed to be.

Latency-Age Children's Understanding of Developmental Disorders

Latency-age children (five to eleven years old) tend to be very industrious, helpful, and eager to earn adult praise. They may feel that behavioral deficiencies on the part of their sibling are partly their fault, and that they should be able to keep the sibling from acting badly. As we discuss in Chapter 6, this belief may be the beginning of the parentified style of coping. Latency-age children believe in fairy tales. Although they may state that Santa Claus is not real, on an emotional level they still very much believe in miracles. Knowing this, parents must be aware that the latency-age children may believe that someday their sibling will be normal. Many early-latency-age children have an imaginary friend, and in siblings of developmentally disabled children, that "friend" may be the "normal" persona of their handicapped brother or sister. Parents can help siblings accept realistic expectations of their disabled brother or sister, so they can appreciate progress when it is made, and when they play a role in its being made.

Latency-age children often compartmentalize their feelings, so it can be difficult to know exactly what they think or feel about their disabled sibling: On one occasion, I attended a sibling support group for five- to ten-year-old brothers of siblings with Cornelia de Lange syndrome. (This is a disorder associated with multiple congenital defects, including occasional missing digits or partly formed limbs and dwarfism, as well as mental retardation.) The group facilitator was trying desperately to get these boys to describe their views of their siblings, but they only wanted to talk about a recent Batman movie. Finally, some description started; an anatomical comparison of their brothers' and sisters' number of missing fingers! It may be difficult for latency-age children to put into words just how their sibling is different, even though they are aware of very real differences.

Conclusions

We have enumerated many factors that influence how well a family is likely to be able to cope with a handicapped child. Coping factors form the context in which the adjustment of the non-handicapped siblings will occur. Although much of how well a sibling is likely to cope can be predicted from the child's position in the family (as discussed in Chapter 2), and from how well the parents accept the handicapped child (as discussed in this chapter), a third set of factors relates to how the child's handicap is viewed and responded to by those around the family. In the next chapter, we examine the effect of culture and other extrafamilial factors on how families with disabled children cope.

Chapter 4

Cultural, Religious, and Educational Factors Influencing Family Adjustment

Many support factors come from within the immediate and extended family of the child born with a developmental disorder. In Chapter 3, we focused on those types of support factors. In addition, some families experience significant help (or sometimes increased difficulty) because of support factors that are part of the environment of their everyday living, but not part of the makeup of the family. We refer to these factors here as *extrafamilial support factors,* which include culture, religion, and educational advantage and how they affect a family's ability to cope successfully.

In writing this chapter, we have formed a composite impression from working with many families from diverse backgrounds. We wish not to create cultural stereotypes, but to reflect on our observations of numerous families, and to convey the working knowledge of trained professionals who specialize in serving specific communities where the beliefs and practices of a particular cultural or ethnic group are dominant.

Different Cultures and Different Attitudes toward the Developmentally Disabled

When a family experiences the birth of a handicapped child, part of its reaction and ability to adapt comes from its preexisting understanding and beliefs about the nature of developmental handicaps. If you are the sibling of a handicapped person, it may not be possible for you to recall a time when you were *not* aware of the existence of handicapped people. Even professionals who work with children and adults with developmental handicaps find it difficult to think back to the time before they had any professional training in, awareness of, or interest in helping the disabled, and to recall what they knew or felt when they saw a developmentally disabled person. Most people who have any degree of formal knowledge about developmental disabilities learned it either in school, in on-the-job training, or from professionals who educated them in how to deal with a disabled family member. But most of the world doesn't deal daily with the developmentally disabled and is only vaguely aware that there *are* handicapped people around. Given this state of affairs, most people have only hazy or partly informed ideas about developmental disorders until a disabled child is born into their family. These ideas constitute a kind of folk wisdom about handicapped people that becomes intermixed with knowledge that the parents gain from educators and doctors about how to deal with their child's difficulty. But as the newly acquired knowledge intermixes with the old folk wisdom, a distinctive pattern of culturally specific attitudes toward disability emerges.

Mainstream Culture and Changing Attitudes toward Developmental Disabilities

When we first diagnose a child with mental retardation, the parents often say that they've never really known someone who's mentally retarded. Of course, virtually all Americans have seen on the street a person with Down's syndrome, but they are probably less aware when they encounter a mentally retarded person who does not have recognizable dysmorphic (atypical) features like a person with Down's syndrome. Lacking formal knowledge and awareness of the developmentally disabled, people dealing with a handicap emerging in their child are confronted by all sorts of folk wisdom about developmental disorders. This folk wisdom falls into three broad classes: (1) the "why this happened to you" category; (2) the "how to make her or him act right" category; and (3) the "what this person will be like when he's older" category.

In American culture, we've seen some very positive changes in how the developmentally disabled are viewed since the early 1960s. Through the 1950s, very little was developed in the way of compensatory education for the cognitively handicapped because it wasn't mandatory for such services to be provided by the public schools. Children recognized as having severe handicaps, such as children who were obviously dysmorphic or deformed at birth, were assumed to be severely retarded. The quality standard of medical practice at that time was to help families with the decision to place such a baby in an institution, to forget the baby as much as possible, and to get on with their lives, that is, to have another baby soon. Many parents did as they were told, and probably, if they believed strongly enough in the infallibility of doctors, were able to live with their decisions relatively well.

Over time, as it became possible to correct medically some of the congenital defects associated with mental retardation syndromes, as in the surgical repair of the heart defects associated with Down's syndrome, or to prevent cognitive impairment through the perinatal screening and dietary treatment of children with phenylketonuria (PKU), some of the children did much better than expected and lived longer. As earlier and more intensive interventions were tried, other children also progressed much more than predicted. Over time, the professional trend was to recommend special education while the child stayed at home, rather than institutionalization as soon as the developmental disorder was diagnosed. In fact, the pendulum has swung completely: Many parents today express a fear that professionals will prescribe institutionalization, and they state in advance of agreeing to any evaluation that they don't want to hear that. The fact of the matter today is that such prescriptions are virtually never made, except for profoundly retarded, medically fragile babies, and there is a significant trend toward keeping even those babies at home.

Today, Americans know it is "politically correct" to display an accepting attitude toward handicapped persons, but this attitude is generally not what families with developmentally disabled members experience. Even though there are ramps and handicap-accessible rest rooms everywhere, and the McDonalds Corporation can point to its social responsibility in hiring the developmentally disabled to wipe tables, the parents and siblings of the developmentally disabled often report that they still feel scrutinized when they appear in public with a disabled family member.

In some ways, parents with Down's syndrome children have it the easiest. Their children have a mental retardation syndrome that is widely recognized as "looking retarded" by most Americans, even by people who don't know the term *Down's syndrome.* If you go to the grocery store with your four-year-old Down's girl in the grocery cart and she pulls six boxes of Cheerios off the shelf, people will look at you sympathetically and help you put back the fallen boxes. If you go to the market with your little boy who looks normal but is in the same special-education class as the little Down's girl, and *he* pulls down the Cheerios, people will look at you as if you are a rotten parent who can't control his or her wild kid. So, much of the stigma that accrues to the parents of developmentally disabled children in our culture comes from the fact that many handicapping conditions are unseen (unlike that of a child in a wheelchair or of one who is obviously palsied). Because badly behaved children are presumed to be far more common than developmentally disabled ones, the public tends to make the more likely attribution, which stigmatizes the parents of the developmentally disabled as "bad" parents.

The Pitfalls of Accepting Stigma

The stigma of being made to feel like a bad parent because your developmentally disabled child acts badly is hard to counteract. Probably the most detrimental aspect is that parents of developmentally disabled children really begin to wonder if they *are* bad parents; whether if they were more adequate parents, their child *wouldn't* pull down cereal boxes in the market. On one level, it is enticing to believe that you, as the parent, *are* at fault because the belief implies that, if you change your behavior, the child's inappropriate behavior can be made to go away. There are many behaviors that a well-informed parent of a handicapped child can be helped to deal with, but realistically, if the child is ten and has a mental age of three, it is reasonable only to expect the child to act like a well-behaved three-year-old.

Cognitive versus Physical Handicaps

Families with a cognitively handicapped family member are usually much less recognizable when they are out in public than are families with a physically handicapped child. People may stare at or avoid a child in a wheelchair, but developmentally disabled children do not call attention to themselves until they act weird or bad. For family members who are around the child all the time, it becomes difficult to know just how normal their child does or does not appear to others. As families get more used to the atypical behavior of the handicapped child, they are likely to feel hostility toward people who stare at their child or show disapproval of the child when the child is, in the family member's opinion, still acting fairly normally. Some families successfully cope with this form of stigma by actually marking the child as handicapped so that people will hopefully be more generous in their evaluations of the child. Forms of self-imposed markers for the cognitively disabled child include putting the child in an extra large stroller (the kind that fits a child up to seven or eight years old) or putting a medical alert bracelet on the child to indicate subtly that this child has some sort of "condition." One mother I met a number of years ago carried brochures from the National Society for Autistic Children with her. If people stared at her child's odd behavior in a store, she'd hand them a brochure.

Although many U.S. families experience stigma for having a developmentally handicapped child, the stigma is most administered by people who are not consciously reacting in a pejorative way because the child has a disability. U.S. culture is altruistic, and when aware that a child is disabled, many people are accommodating and helpful. Parents experience this, too. As will be discussed later, the United States supports one of the most extensive networks of educational and family services for the developmentally disabled, so in this culture, acknowledging the difficulties of families with disabled children and making a commitment to help are valued. In other cultures, views differ somewhat, depending on beliefs about culpability for the child's disabilities.

Asian Families and Developmental Disabilities

In our clinic, we serve a diversity of families from different cultural groups. Because our clinic is at the University of California, San Francisco, we see numerous families of Asian origin, mostly with immigrant or first-generation parents. (San Francisco is the most Asian city, by percentage, of any city in the United States.) Mental health and educational professionals, including many who themselves are Asian, acknowledge that working with Asian families is often difficult and frustrating. On average, Asian children are brought in later for first visits, although the parents will subsequently describe their awareness of the child's problems from a very early age.

The "why did this happen to me" folk wisdom that was mentioned earlier seems to play a major role in the adaptation of many Asian families to accepting the presence of a developmental disability in a child. For Asian families, there seems to be much more shame associated with having a developmentally disabled child. For a long time, I struggled to understand this. Then, on one occasion, I was given at least one explanation by the Indonesian-Chinese aunt of an autistic boy. "In Buddhism," she said, "the belief is that if you get away with making money illegally (perhaps other undesirable acts are included here as well), your misdeeds will be manifest to others nonetheless—in the form of a disabled child. Therefore, having a disabled child is something to hide. It shows everyone that you are not the good person you appear to be." It is unclear how overt or widespread this belief is in Asian families, but it certainly seems to be a reasonable explanation of why Asian parents often seem reluctant to seek or use special services for their children. Asian parents also tend to lack an interest in joining support groups and more often than other families refuse one-to-one introductions to another Asian family who has a similarly disabled child slightly older (a service we often provide in our clinic for families that feel they might benefit from a more experienced shoulder to lean on).

Once a diagnosis is made, denial of the severity of the child's disability seems most obvious in Asian families. This denial takes several forms: Several mothers whose children we follow insist that the children say many words that no one else but the mothers can understand. Often in such cases the mothers report the use of phrases that don't make sense linguistically (but do emotionally) such as "I love you, Mommy," said by a child who can not yet point correctly to a picture of a cat as opposed to a dog. In general, we see many Asian parents who feel that their child is understanding everything said to him or her, whereas testing reveals that the child really understands very little (even when tested in both English and his or her own dialect). Some parents read more preferences and intentionality into their child's activities than others, like "choosing" music to listen to by letting a hand fall into a box of cassettes and then, with help, retrieving the one he or she was "trying to get." Of course, it is not possible for a doctor who sees a child for only a few hours at a time to know everything about what a child can and cannot do. It is possible only to compare across children, and to make observations about how different parents try, in different ways, to compensate for their child's problems.

The Special Role of the Asian Mother

In most Asian families, it is clear that the mother is designated as the primary and usually the sole child rearer. The father is more often absent than fathers from other cultural groups, from evaluations and participation in treatment, and from meetings with the school. On the other hand, the mother more than compensates, often doing things beyond what mothers from other cultural groups do, and can be fairly described as taking quite a martyred stance.

One Chinese mother, Mrs. Tan, whose ten-year-old boy, Jerry, I've known since age four, spent one year with him in Japan because she had decided that was the best program for him. During the following two years, Mrs. Tan enrolled Jerry in school in Boston, 3,000 miles from home, living there with him. Mrs. Tan now has Jerry in a private school close to her home, where he is the only pupil in his class and gets large amounts of one-to-one instruction. On their most recent visit, I met the Tans' other son for the first time, a high-school-aged young man. Mrs. Tan had taken him out of school that day to come to the visit with her. This young man was extremely parentified in his attitude toward Jerry, and he was socially awkward. I wondered how well he was doing in his own socialization, and what importance he placed on his own needs.

Another Chinese family we follow, the Fongs, have two autistic boys and have enrolled their sons in the same school in Boston that Jerry Tan has attended. Mrs. Fong has set up a second household in Boston. The family's first home is in Manila. Mr. Fong goes back and forth. Again, one worries about the emotional toll of this lifestyle on both parents.

Mrs. Young's boy, Frank, a severely retarded autistic child, spent two years in a private school that his school district refused to reimburse the family for because it claimed its own program was "appropriate." Mrs. Young persisted in her appeals for reimbursement to the federal appeals court level. The day of the federal appeals court hearing, her attorney announced first thing that Mrs. Young could not attend because she had been hospitalized the night before for chest pains. My thought was how sad it was that this mother felt she had to kill herself for this boy.

Obviously, there are good and bad points in parents that go to these extremes. Their dedication to their children is incredible. They will do anything, no matter how hard, no matter how many hours a day it takes, no matter if the child makes less progress than they may have wished. As in Mrs. Young's experience, this dedication takes a personal toll. As in Mrs. Tan's case, there is reason to be worried about the longer term psychological development of the siblings, who get left behind physically or emotionally for years while all the effort goes into the disabled child.

Sometimes family members will be very specific in attributing the "cause" of a child's disability. An example is the case of Aaron Erikson, who came for his visit from Jakarta, accompanied by his mother and his maternal grandmother. His mother was Chinese, his father Scandinavian. Aaron's grandmother sat quietly through the genetic and obstetric history designed to screen for possible causes of the child's disorder. At the end of the evaluation, when asked if she had any questions, the grandmother simply stated that it was clear that what was wrong was that Aaron had mixed blood, and this outcome was what was to be expected (the "what caused it" folk wisdom). There seemed to be a sad sense of fate or destiny in the grandmother's pronouncement that made me wonder whether she believed treatment could really help her grandson. From such interactions as mine with that grandmother it may be difficult to tell what these grandmothers say to their daughters in private, as well as how much familial support and help is physically or emotionally available in such circumstances. Certainly the feeling that a child's fate is sealed is a depressing prospect.

Latino Families and Developmental Disabilities

Another cultural group with distinctive ways of reacting to having a developmentally disabled child is Latinos. As in the Asian families, the father's role in child rearing is usually more peripheral than in other American families, but the effect of a developmentally disabled child on the father's sense of family pride is usually more obvious, especially if the handicapped child is a son, and particularly a first son. One positive way in which Latino families often cope, is in having more children. In non-Hispanic families a "stoppage" rule is often in effect. (*Stoppage* is a genetic term used in calculating the risk of recurring handicaps in a family, and it refers to the probability that a family will stop having children after they realize that one child is disabled in some way.) Hispanic families tend to have more children, who make the family environment more normal, who broadly share in the care of the handicapped child, and who lessen the parental sense of failure over having produced a child with a disability.

The Madonna Syndrome: Latino Mothers

One significant drawback that I've encountered repeatedly in Latino families can be illustrated most vividly by the case of Genicia Rios. Genicia has Rett's syndrome, a degenerative neurological condition that affects only girls. In Rett's syndrome, after a period of normal development, there is often a regression back to about a six- to twelve-month-old level of functioning, including loss of the ability to walk and a functional loss of the use of the hands, which are almost continually engaged in a hand-wringing movement. I had first seen Genicia when she was a very cute little two-and-a-half-year-old in a lacy pink dress who appeared to be moderately retarded. At that time, her father held her and carried her almost constantly, and it was clear that he was very attached to her. By the time she was nine, she was losing ambulation and walked only if pushed; she would then stagger until she could make herself come to a halt. She was not toilet-trained and could not feed herself neatly. Her father worked long hours, and her mother was solely responsible for Genicia's physical care. I talked privately to Mrs. Rios, who told me she couldn't handle the burden of care anymore. She said that it was a very painful realization, but that she wanted to see Genicia placed in a residential care facility. Later, while Mrs. Rios played with Genicia in our playroom, Mr. Rios and I watched her from behind a one-way mirror.

I asked Mr. Rios what he though about possible residential placement for Genicia. He said, "My wife is a madonna. She is the only one who can care for Genicia well enough." He loved and admired his wife but could not acknowledge her pain.

In cases such as Genicia's, the family structure is strong, and there is usually a lot of extended-family contact and support. The parents' time spent with siblings and in-laws keeps them from feeling isolated, and the disabled child's many cousins keep him or her from being raised isolated. Behavioral standards for the children are often not as strict as, say, in Asian families, so developmentally disabled behavior is less often seen as "bad" behavior. The burden does, however, fall heavily on one parent, the mother, and she is trapped into being the sole person responsible for the child because she is idealized in the very situation that she, ironically, feels she is handling most poorly: as a mother. In discussing treatment recommendations with Latino mothers, we often feel that they have a sense of hopelessness that they can ever help their child by implementing various suggestions. Sometimes, the reason is that the mother does not speak English and knows she's up against an English-speaking school, English-speaking therapists and so on. Sometimes, the reason is that the family is without many economic resources, even though we've seen other families without economic resources take a very self-sufficient attitude toward helping their child change. The reaction of Latino mothers to the diagnosis of a developmental disorder seems to go beyond language or economic barriers into a larger state of helplessness. For example, no one in our clinic would have placed favorable odds on Mrs. Rios's prevailing on her husband to have Genicia placed any time soon.

African-American Families and Developmental Disabilities

The African-American families we see have some distinct advantages in coping with a developmentally disabled sibling that are absent in some of the other cultural groups that I have described. The extended family tends to be a tremendous resource, and many parents come to clinic visits with their own parents or their own siblings, and with their other children who come along as helpers.

Many of the benefits that larger families experience when they try to cope with developmentally disabled children are found in African-American families that live with or near relatives who share in the care of a larger group of children. Often, siblings are imbued with a sense of the importance of watching out for younger brothers and sisters, and almost all siblings, younger or older, will watch out for a handicapped child. One advantage that siblings in African-American families often have is that their parents are willing to vest disciplinary authority in them. So if a ten-year-old brother sees his three-year-old hyperactive retarded brother run for the street, he'll grab him and swat his bottom (and not wait until he can find his mother to do it). This authority to take action is good, because if the ten-year-old waits until he finds his mother and explains what happened, the three-year-old will have forgotten what he did wrong.

For reasons that are unclear, African-American mothers seem more often than mothers in other cultural groups to describe their developmentally disabled children as successfully "hanging out" with a larger group of neighborhood kids. Other parents more often describe their developmentally disabled children as being shamed or just ignored if they try to hang out with other children living nearby. To some extent, siblings try to mediate and buffer their disabled siblings during such playtimes, but there is always a point where the normal sibling gets caught up in what's going on, and the developmentally disabled sibling has to more-or-less go it alone. It is at these times that the more accepting attitude of African-American children seems to come to the fore. Developmentally disabled children can learn many social skills simply by exposure to nonhandicapped peers, so it is an important advantage for disabled children to live in a cultural group where their "difference" is not a basis for rejection. Even though a disabled child may be perceived as "different," he will not automatically be rejected for it.

Religion and How It Helps in Coping with a Disabled Child

Workers in any branch of medical care are aware that a very powerful factor in helping families cope with any sort of dire diagnosis is the family's degree of religious faith. Religious belief is not a panacea for families facing life with a developmentally disabled child, but it does provide some sense of meaning and purpose to a particular family that must cope with a disabled member. In our clinic, many parents mention fundamentalist religious beliefs as giving them a basis for truly believing that they have no reason to feel guilty about their child's having been born disabled, and that it was God's will. Some see raising a handicapped child as a kind of test of their most altruistic traits that will enable them to become more pure through suffering. Others turn to God when the child fails to change, or grows worse, in order to look for a meaning or an explanation. Many religions prescribe specific steps to take, through prayer, meditation, or acts of charity, to achieve change or redemption for the disabled child. This resource may be very useful to a parent who might otherwise feel helpless. Another prime source of support for religious families is that they belong to communities of like-minded people. Many mentally retarded three-year-olds who have been asked to leave their neighborhood preschool are welcome at their church Sunday school. Although Sunday school has a different purpose from preschool, it gives parents a breather and a context for feeling that their child is not a total outcast. When some families start special intensive therapy programs for their disabled children, their church group is a place to which they can turn for volunteers to help carry out the therapy. The Judeo-Christian religious ethic stands against outright discrimination against someone because of the conditions of his or her birth.

An interesting example of how religious faith helps in coping with developmental disability is the case of the Church of Jesus Christ of the Latter-Day Saints (Mormon) in Utah. Utah is approximately 90 percent Mormon, and so the tenets of the Mormon church and how Mormon families live pervade the lifestyle everywhere. Family sizes tend to be large; five children are common, and seven children are not at all unusual. A disabled child is looked on as a destiny and, in certain ways, as the blessing of a particularly pure soul who accepts life even in a disabled body. There is very little stoppage. While working in Utah with families with more than one autistic child, we were amazed to observe that certain "symptoms" of autism were less common. For example, tantrumming over a meal's not being "just so" does not happen in a family where five other children are waiting to get their dinner and will eat your dinner if you don't. There are, quite often, both older siblings to provide supervision and younger siblings to play at the disabled child's developmental level. There are enough siblings so that the burden of the extra care and supervision that the disabled child requires does not fall on only one or two. On a broader level, when most registered voters are the parents of about five children or the grandparents of about twenty-five grandchildren, bonds for education and family services are more heavily supported, and the quality of other extrafamilial support factors is higher.

An example of a young Mormon family we follow in the San Francisco Bay Area demonstrates how a strong religious life can affect what ordinarily would be considered a family at risk, even if they didn't have a developmentally disabled child. Jim and Karen Orleans were still in high school when Karen became pregnant with their first child. They are both Mormons, and they got married right away and moved in with her parents. Karen did not finish high school and the next year had James, Jr., our patient. By the time we first saw James, Jr., at age two and a half, there was a year-old sibling, and Karen was again pregnant. Jim himself had a history of atypical development and learning disabilities and, as a young child, had been a residential treatment patient in our hospital for three years. Jim now was working as a night janitor for the school district. Karen and Jim were twenty-two and twenty-three years old. They were coping very well. Even the most embittered and pessimistic of social workers couldn't have found anything mentally unhealthy about this family. The Orleanses could attribute the strength of their marriage and their ability to parent well to their mutual commitment to their church, and they felt that their numerous progeny were each a blessing. James, Jr., was treated very normally, in that he was neither pushed and primed nor ignored or rejected.

Other families from non-Western cultures and religions may similarly experience their religious values as a binding force in helping to continue family life as normally as possible after the birth of a disabled child. In one of our earlier cases, the Shahs, a Muslim Pakistani family, were living transiently in the United States while Mr. Shah worked for a large multinational computer company. By the time they left, they had learned a great deal about what their autistic son, Jamil, needed in terms of treatment, and they took with them, to their next posting in the Middle East, their own curriculum materials in order to continue Jamil's education themselves. By the time Jamil was ten, Mrs. Shah knew how to teach him, but she could no longer catch Jamil when he (frequently) ran off without warning. This task and many other behavior-management activities were the responsibility of fourteen-year-old Javid, Jamil's older brother, as Javid was the only family member who could run fast enough to catch his brother. About a year after they had settled in the Middle East, I received a very moving letter from the Shahs. First, they said, Jamil's education was going as well as they had expected; they had encountered an unemployed speech-pathologist wife of a British oil-company executive, and she was delighted to have some work tutoring Jamil. They could afford a full-time houseboy to chase Jamil when he ran off. But they were concerned about Javid. They worried that, when they grew older, he would be his brother's only keeper. The Shahs wanted information on the advisability of enlarging their family, so that the ultimate responsibility for Jamil's care would not be Javid's alone. Although their religion and culture dictated strongly that siblings should care for disabled brothers and sisters when the parents no longer could, the Shahs recognized the unfairness of leaving the burden to one child and were willing to take some risk to prevent this.

Thus far, with the exception of Buddhism, which is actually more of a philosophy than a religion, we are aware of no religious groups that shame rather than support families with handicapped children. What all religious families we encounter seem to have in common is a sense of fate or destiny guiding their lives as well as their handicapped child's. In some religions, such as Mormonism, accepting destiny seems to allow a normalization of the disabled child within the family that makes everyone less tense. In other families, religion allows some release from a sense of blame or shame for having an atypical child, freeing the family members to expend their energies in a normal range of activities, rather than in endless attempts to compensate for or deny the child's condition, attempts that result in a distortion of family dynamics.

A Parent's Level of Formal Education and Coping with a Disabled Child

Another major factor in how parents cope with a developmentally disabled child is the parents' level of education. In psychological research, the parental level of education is often used as a "control" variable; that is, it is used as a measure of many different attitudes, beliefs, and behaviors that have already been demonstrated to correlate highly with it. With respect to child rearing, more educated parents are usually easier on children; less educated parents are usually more likely to use strict means of discipline. Better educated parents more often value how smart their child is; less educated parents are more likely to emphasize the importance of good behavior. Similarly, some general trends can be observed in how more and less educated parents tend to deal with developmentally disabled children. These trends can be related to parental permissiveness versus authoritarianism; the ability to understand the nature of the child's disorder and to evaluate the treatment alternatives; a knowledge of consumer rights and the ability to use the available resources; and economic resources.

Parental Education and Parenting Style

Parental level of education is important in understanding parental defenses about the difficulties of living with a developmentally disabled child. One of the most often replicated findings in child development is that more educated parents tend to be more permissive with their children, and that less educated parents tend to be more restrictive. (There are many interesting variations on this theme that bear on culture, the age of the child, and so on, but these go beyond the scope of our present discussion.) Some child psychologists add a third dimension to parenting style that lies between "permissive" and "authoritarian" and is described as "authoritative." Permissive parenting consists of allowing the child to make many of his or her own choices and, hopefully, to learn from his or her own actions. Such parents generally feel that it is best for the child to figure out what to do and when to do it, in order to foster creativity and independent thinking. In the "authoritative" parenting style, the parents define stricter limits for behavior, such as when and where a child may and may not do certain things, but they allow the child to make choices within those limits of acceptability. More restrictive or "authoritarian" parents set firm limits for the behavior they deem appropriate and do not feel it necessary that the child understand why the parent has set those limits; the child understands only that acceptability is predicated on being able to readily and willingly follow parental rules.

All other things being equal, these methods of parenting produce, approximately, the desired results. However, when the child has a developmental disorder, especially a severe one, the premises about children on which these parenting styles are based become invalid. Parents with a permissive style generally have the hardest time adapting to the methods that are usually more suitable to raising a developmentally disabled child. Because the child is cognitively handicapped, her or his exploration tends to be more limited—that is, more brief, more repetitive, or more one-dimensional—than that of another child of the same age. Therefore, the philosophy of allowing the child to learn through his or her own choices works less well, and the opportunities to exhibit inappropriate behavior are greater. The highly permissive parent who takes the child's inappropriate behavior as "his own style" further attenuates the child's opportunities to move on. For example, Jeremy, a four-year-old autistic boy, had parents who both had graduate degrees. His mother had an art-related import business. When Jeremy started lining up and otherwise arranging crayons, she refused to intervene, even when he stared and flapped his hands at the crayons for prolonged periods. She felt that his activity was part of a unique creative process that he was experimenting with. Although she was advised that many autistic children line up sets of like objects, and that such perseverative behavior interferes with being exposed to broader forms of stimulation, she felt it would be unfair to Jeremy to interfere with his behavior.

Other examples are less benign: Ansel, a six-year-old boy (the only child of older parents), was brought to be evaluated by his impeccably suited, erudite publisher father and his mother, the curator-director of a small museum. One problem we saw was that Ansel abruptly approached his father, grabbed his beautifully made silk tie, and pulled it until his father's face began to redden. Another problem was that, when aggravated, Ansel would pull down his pants and threaten to urinate on the floor—and sometimes did. Much to my amazement, Ansel's parents made no attempt to stop either of these behaviors; rather, they attended to him urgently and gently, as they took these behaviors to mean that he was quite unhappy about something, and that the onus was on them to figure out what—right away. As I worked with these parents to implement some methods that would be effective in stopping these behaviors and redirecting them into more appropriate ways of requesting attention and help, it became clear how counterintuitive a more restrictive approach to child rearing was to them. Had this couple had a son of their own high level of intelligence, rather than a boy with severe receptive and expressive language impairments, their methods probably *would* have fostered the development of a creative, independent child cast in their own image. The very permissive method of child rearing contrasts completely with the more structured interventions that benefit many developmentally disabled children, such as intensive behavior therapy. Thus, it is often harder for more educated parents, who tend toward permissive child-rearing methods, to cope with the demands of parenting a developmentally disabled child.

A resulting problem is that more educated, more permissive parents often find themselves trapped in a morass of conflicting parenting values. If these parents follow a doctor's or a teacher's advice and set more limits for their developmentally disabled child and are able to do it in such a way that the results are desirable, they begin to adhere to a more restrictive method of parenting for that child. As time goes on, these parents realize that they need to hold the disabled child to stricter behavior limits than her or his nonhandicapped siblings. Unless they recognize this need, the nondisabled siblings will develop a pervasive sense of injustice when behaviorally and developmentally unwarranted restrictions are imposed on their behavior because of the parents' attempt to be fair to all of their children.

Parents with an authoritative style of child rearing usually find it easier to understand the value of imposing a fairly high degree of structure on a child with problems in learning. Although behavior modification programs may not be the preferred way for such parents to go (e.g., putting sticker charts on the refrigerator and giving pieces of popcorn for "Good work!"), there is usually a fairly easy adaptation. Although the subject has never been formally studied, such parents seem to have an easier time striking a balance in setting separate rules for their disabled and their normally developing children.

An interesting case is authoritarian parents. Educators and doctors are accustomed to thinking that less educated, more authoritarian parents are not as "optimal" as other parents in structuring learning experiences for their children. As it happens, when it comes to learning how to provide a highly structured, routinized, "do it over until you get it right" environment, authoritarian parents do it quite naturally. In our clinic, we see quite a few families referred to us from the U.S. Army's Exceptional Families program, which provides services for military families with developmentally disabled children. It is difficult to discern whether families that join the military have an authoritarian bent, or whether the military makes them that way. In either case, military personnel, both fathers and mothers, have no trouble understanding or accepting the fact that their developmentally disabled child needs to learn to follow narrowly defined directives when requested. Drill and repetition are OK with them, too. An additional advantage of more authoritarian families in simultaneously parenting both disabled and nondisabled children is that they tend to set simple rules—rules that can be understood and followed by both the normal and the nonhandicapped children. For example, the Bentons, a Marine family, had four boys, ages four, three, one-and-a-half, and six months. The three older boys, including the mildly mentally retarded four-year-old, were running around the clinic playroom one day, shouting and "shooting" each other with toy guns and sticks. Their dad's response to the chaos was one simple rule: "Hey! Don't point those guns at anyone."

In teaching the principles of behavior modification, most behavior therapists have an easier time with more authoritarian, less educated parents than with highly educated, permissive parents, who tend to resist until the benefit of this approach is somehow shown to them.

An interesting case of relevance here is the single-parent father of a severely retarded mute boy, Roy, whom we followed for a number of years. Roy's father, Mr. Naylor, was a very large man with a bushy beard who had a Harley-Davidson motorcycle repair business and a large tattoo on his upper arm indicating membership in the Northern California Hell's Angels. On one visit when Roy was nine, the conversation was interrupted by Roy banging loudly on a toy xylophone. Mr. Naylor and I were talking about the likelihood that his son would learn to speak. In frustration, because he could not hear me well over the sound of the xylophone, Mr. Naylor roughly yanked the xylophone away from Roy, shouting "Cut the shit!" About a minute later, Mr. Naylor returned the xylophone to Roy. A minute after that, Roy was banging again (but not quite so loudly). His father again removed the xylophone and repeated his admonition. The third time he used the xylophone, Roy tinkled quietly and appropriately on the keys, and nothing further was said. Although a behavior therapist would not have recommended exactly the same procedure, Mr. Naylor's natural style of parenting bore a striking resemblance, in both methodology and results, to a plan that might have been developed by a behavior therapist to reduce Roy's tendency to produce overly loud sounds. The natural style of parenting of a relatively unschooled, authoritarian father like Mr. Naylor was quite effective with his boy, and on his own, he was able to cope with problem behaviors without feeling he had tampered with his value system for raising children.

Parental Education and Acceptance of the Diagnosis

Most highly educated parents easily can intellectually comprehend the diagnosis of a developmental disorder and the ramifications of etiology and prognosis. However, a preponderance of well-educated parents seem to have difficulty accepting the diagnosis of a developmental disorder. Although less educated parents may understand less about etiology, diagnosis, and treatment, they generally find it easier to accept the idea that a disability is present (and that the family will need to develop ways to cope with it). There seem to be a variety of reasons for this difference.

Often, more educated parents have more elaborate defenses for deflecting them from the painful truth that their child has a lifelong disability. Very educated professionals who are the parents of a child with a developmental disorder may seek second, third, and fourth opinions about their child's diagnosis. Whenever something slightly different is said to them, they may interpret it as completely contradictory to the last opinion, perpetuating the illusion that no one understands anything about what is wrong with the child. When this type of denial and rejection of the child's diagnosis is looked at in the context of the rest of the family's functioning, there may be an overall detrimental effect—not only on the child, who needs to have some sort of treatment, but on other family members as well. Everything else, all other family issues, are often put on hold until the parents can accept a complete explanation of their child's problem.

Another reason that educated parents sometimes have more difficulty dealing with a developmental disorder is that the parents' own educational level and occupational status are far above what they may hope for their child. It is painfully hard for a father who is a lawyer to picture his son as a gardener's assistant. However, if the father is a gardener, having a son who grows up to be a gardener's assistant isn't so bad. The gardener father may also hope for sons who will become lawyers, but the son who does not achieve far more than he has achieved does not cause the same wound to his pride. When the nonhandicapped siblings show promise of a level of achievement similar to that of the parents, the intellectual gap between siblings of nearly the same age is all the more apparent. In order to psychologically narrow the gap (which constantly stresses how far behind the developmentally disabled child is), the parent must either minimize the achievements of the normal child or deny evidence of the limitations of the disabled child.

Conclusions

It is clear that families cope with a developmentally disabled child differently, and that how each family copes depends on a complex set of variables, including the personalities of all involved; the number, gender, and spacing of the other siblings; and the family's cultural setting. In the next chapter, we discuss aspects of the intra-psychic, internal psychological processes that help individuals cope with a disabled family member. Various defense mechanisms help both parents and siblings to protect themselves from some of the painful realities associated with a family life made more demanding by a child with special needs.

Chapter 5

Coping and Defending: Applying the Adult- Children-of-Alcoholics Model

Children tend to learn their parents' coping style and approach to problems. If the parents feel cheated, depressed, angry, and resentful about their plight, then the children will tend to feel the same way. Such emotions may extend to or be displaced onto other situations, thus becoming almost reflexive or automatic whenever difficulties arise later in life.

Parents' tendency to misplace anger toward others and to feel helpless will become the legacy that they leave behind. On the other hand, a more positive, honest problem-solving approach to each difficulty that comes up can be the gift they pass along. It is the children of these parents who have a better chance of becoming adults who reflect fondly on their childhood. They will be able to claim legitimately that having a disabled sibling is the reason for many of their positive traits as adults.

In attempting to provide a helpful model for understanding how parents and their children deal with a developmentally disabled child in the family, we make some comparisons between the situations faced by adult siblings who grew up with a developmentally disabled sibling and the literature on adult children of alcoholics (ACOAs). The reason we chose the alcoholism literature is that the vast majority of the books in the lay press deal with alcoholism. The same principles apply to other addictions or to any other stressor that takes the family's energies away. However, with both alcoholism and autism, you are dealing with a situation in which someone's behavior is a family problem; that is, someone's unpredictable behavior is a source of free-floating anxiety and embarrassment.

Examples of the books available are *Recovery: A Guide for Adult Children of Alcoholics,* by Herbert L. Gravitz and Julie Bowden; *Learning to Love Yourself,* by Sharon Wegscheider-Cruse; *Struggle for Intimacy,* by Janet Geringer-Wolitz; and *The Family,* by John Bradshaw.

The Adult-Children-of-Alcoholics (ACOA) Model

Since the mid-1980s, there has been a virtual explosion of written material about the adult children of alcoholics. Walk into any bookstore, and you are likely to see a large section dedicated to this and related topics, usually right alongside the sections on traditional psychology and pop psychology. Initially, these books dealt solely with the impact of alcoholism on a family, especially on those adults who spent their childhood in this environment. The description of such adults as "OK on the outside yet troubled on the inside" strikes a resonant chord in many. The difficulties that these people experience include alcoholism, frequent bouts of depression, low self-esteem, and various emotional and psychosomatic illnesses. More recently, these books have increased their base to include those who have come from other troubled backgrounds, for example, *My Parents' Keeper,* by Eva Brown, for those who were raised by a mentally ill parent, and *Healing the Child Within,* by Charles Whitfield, for those who grew up in a "dysfunctional home."

It is important for us to acknowledge that many of the "maladaptive" coping mechanisms adopted by ACOAs apply to those who grew up with a handicapped sibling. Unfortunately, much of the language used is still based on chemical dependency and on the twelve-step programs that are helpful to so many. This language does not apply to most people who are reading this book.

One term born out of the ACOA movement is *codependency*. This is the disease of those who "facilitate" the other person's alcoholism. So much of the codependents' lives revolves around the person with the disease that they learn to sacrifice many of their own needs to those of the alcoholic. Often, the same dynamics occur in those who are living with a disabled person.

We realize that, in many ways, developmental disorders in children are a far cry from alcoholism, and that the mere implication of a similarity may be offensive to some. The specifics of the problem are indeed different, but as implied in Chapter 1, there is a similarity in the effects on a family; here, it isn't the disease or disorder itself but simply its presence and effects that result in family dysfunction. For example, in the case of alcoholism the codependents are considered "enablers" because their behavior allows the alcoholic to continue to deny his or her disease and thus prolong it. In most instances, the disabled child's "disease process" is not "enabled" by a codependent family member. The effect on the family member(s), however, is often the same because the family is, to a greater or lesser extent, centered on the needs and behavior of one person. This dynamic is potentially dangerous for the emotional well-being of all the other family members; that is, their growth and development play second fiddle to their dealing with the disabled child. In the case of autism or mental retardation, a codependent family member may be reluctant to institute behavioral modification or apply any form of discipline. Because some of the negative characteristics of the child's handicap are not identified and dealt with, as such, they are "enabled" (i.e., allowed to exist and maybe even to become more ingrained).

Below are some of the classic characteristics seen in the adult children of alcoholics. Because of similar family dynamics, "adult siblings" are also likely to take on many of the same characteristics.

High Responsibility

Very early in life, the siblings of a disabled child often have to take care of—or, at the very least, participate in the care of— someone who is ill. If they are not participating directly in the care, their lives are certainly affected by those who are physically or emotionally absent because of increased responsibilities. Often, when siblings are asked to take on caretaking roles, they are asked to do so at a level that exceeds appropriate expectations for their chronological age. A younger sibling often takes on the role of older sibling. To refuse to do so is to risk being called selfish or uncaring.

Denial of the Right to Be Childlike

Because of this high degree of responsibility early in life, these children frequently lose out on what is usually a carefree and untroubled time. As in the alcoholic family, where emotional resources and reserves are already depleted, here, too, the family's ability to cope is stretched to the limit. Parents have little patience for any mischief or normal "childish" activity. The healthy siblings of an autistic child are expected to look out for him or her (e.g., while out playing) and are thus further deprived of a more relaxed, more "normal" childhood.

Placing One's Own Needs Second

Because of the years spent placing another's needs ahead of their own, these children often learn always to place their own needs second. Considering themselves first often causes feelings of guilt. This is a manifestation of "survivor guilt" and may become a lifetime habit. A sibling feels that it could easily have been he or she who was born with the disability and may consciously or unconsciously feel guilty for being healthy.

Emotional Vulnerabilities

Statistically, those who grew up with alcoholism and those who grew up with a disabled sibling are all vulnerable to certain types of emotional disturbances, such as alcoholism, eating disorders, divorce, and chronic depression. Once again, the disease process is different, but the potential manifestations in the mental and emotional health of the families of developmentally disabled children may be quite similar, although this topic has not yet been explicitly studied.

Difficulties in Forming Friendships

Inviting friends home becomes a potential source of embarrassment and may require the child to share something very personal, whether she or he is ready to do so or not. In the case of alcoholism, the child is at the mercy of the parent's drinking behavior, which is often unpredictable. In the case of a developmentally disabled child, the afflicted family member's behavior may also be unpredictable. In either case, the unpredictability is a potential source of anxiety, pain, and embarrassment. Mary Strand, age sixteen, has an autistic brother Michael, age eighteen. Her parents report that Mary refuses to have girlfriends visit anymore because six-foot-tall Michael appeared naked, and with an erection, in the living room when he heard his sister and her friend laughing and giggling there. Afterward, in discussing with Mary what had happened, the parents knew that when Mary said she "understood" Michael's behavior, she didn't mean that it was OK. At that point, the Strands began to seriously consider residential placement for Michael.

One who has a difficult time making and maintaining friendships early in life may have similar difficulties later as well. Therefore, taking steps to make it easier for a child to invite friends home is crucial. We discuss this subject further in Chapter 10.

Familial Melancholy and Tension

When one family member's behavior is difficult to control, and one gets the feeling that, no matter what one does, the outcome will remain the same, the result may be "learned helplessness," in which one loses hope and gives up trying to effect positive change. In the face of learned helplessness, melancholy hangs in the air and most children will pick up on it and internalize it. When so much revolves around the unpredictable behavior of a single family member, free-floating tension and anxiety may result. Siblings often describe a feeling of "walking on eggshells." This chronic tension may have long-term consequences.

The Specter of an Uncertain Future

Disabilities such as autism and many forms of mental retardation that are not associated with health-related congenital defects raise the specter of an uncertain future that may be more stressful than when one is living with an alcoholic or with a physically disabled child who has less than full life expectancy. For all intents and purposes, the sibling with, for example, autism will be present for the duration of one's life, and this difficult fact must be faced sooner or later. (Concrete ways of dealing with this problem are discussed in Chapter 11.)

"It's in the Will"

Warren Caldwell, age thirty-three, is a successful attorney on the West Coast. He grew up with a younger autistic brother, Henry, now age twenty-eight. So concerned were their parents that Henry would be left on his own after they died that they had it written in their will that Warren was required to visit his brother a set number of times each year. Warren deeply resented this stipulation. He had no problem visiting his brother and had every intention of doing so, but the idea of being legally bound to do so left a sour taste in his mouth. It implied that his parents didn't trust his assurances. Henry was recently placed in a home for autistic adults, and Warren was sorry that his brother had not been placed earlier. In addition to being healthier for the family, the earlier placement also would also have been healthier for Henry. Looking back, Warren feels that growing up with the family gave Henry a false picture of what his adult life would be like. Henry had been very pampered at home and lacked the independent living skills he needed to adjust well in a group home. Earlier placement would have been better for Warren, who would have received the attention he deserved from his parents. Once, when interviewed by the local paper, his mother had claimed that having Henry in the house had brought the family closer together. After reading this statement, Warren recalls, he resented it for years: "It simply wasn't true. It didn't bring our family closer together at all!"

With an alcoholic parent or a sibling with a disorder that shortens life expectancy, one is eventually independent. Those with an autistic or mentally retarded sibling feel pressure, implied or direct, that the burden of care will fall to them once their parents are gone. Some of this burden is relieved with the improved options now available, such as group homes. However, much has to be done in the way of financial arrangements, conservatorships, and so on, which makes it difficult to plan for an independent future.

Marital Relationships

The marital relationship of the parents is strained similarly by either alcoholism or a disabled child (as discussed in Chapter 3). In either case, the parents have far less than optimal emotional energy for their children. Also, the parents may not cope in the same way: One may be in denial while the other is more realistic. This difference may further strain their relationship. Parents may, and often do, have different ideas about the appropriate management of the disabled child. Marital strain over the care of a disabled child, like marital strain over the management of a spouse's alcoholism, tends to produce a family life that is less than ideal for the other siblings.

Although this subject has not been specifically studied, the marriages of the adult siblings of disabled children, like those of the adult children of alcoholics, may be unstable, especially if there was significant marital strain in the family of origin. Not only may these people grow up with chronic difficulties in forming healthy relationships, but any caretaking responsibilities that they have to take on as adults hold the potential for conflict in a marriage.

Denial

> "It was the first time I let myself think that there was something wrong with Randall," he said to me as he stacked and restacked the photographs. "And what I remember most vividly is the relief, the letting go of all the denial." (Sue Miller, *Family Pictures*)

Denial can be defined as avoiding the awareness of some painful reality. Virtually everyone has used this mechanism at some point. Denial may even be helpful in allowing one to survive the immediate effects of trauma. For example, in dealing with a death in the family, some degree of denial allows a relative to make funeral plans and get other affairs in order. In fact, people often report that the reality of the death "didn't hit me until a week later, when life settled back to normal."

In the short run, denial may be an ally, but in the long run, it is almost always a foe. In the case of alcoholism, the problem being denied may be manifested quietly or dramatically. It is easy to see how some of the subtle manifestations of autism and other developmental disorders can be denied especially before a formal diagnosis is made. In the short run, denial may be effective in allowing the gradual acceptance of a painful reality. If denial persists, however, it will interfere with the acceptance of and the adjustment to important realities in relation to both the affected child and the other siblings. And, as previously mentioned, one parent's being in denial will have negative implications for the marriage and the whole family's adjustment.

While we most often think of denial in terms of how it prevents parents from acting realistically about their handicapped child's limitations, denial may also misguide siblings. Siblings may have very active fantasies about their brother's or sister's being normal someday. They imagine him or her being just like them. It is important for the whole family to see the handicapped child's problem realistically so that reality as well as fantasy motivates the love and caring that siblings direct toward their disabled brother or sister. When parental denial is very strong, the siblings may know next to nothing about what is really wrong with their brother or sister. In the absence of real information, confusing, frightening, or guilty beliefs may arise.

A sibling who grows up in an environment in which denial is the primary defense mechanism has literally been trained to distrust his or her own observations and instincts. The result may be an insecure adult who depends on others to make decisions and who keeps feelings to himself or herself.

Inconsistency or "Crisis Mode"

The parents of a disabled child are often absorbed, preoccupied, and worried; they feel helpless. This feeling of helplessness may cause them to be irritable and impatient in dealing with their healthy children because they have such low emotional reserves. As a result, love and understanding are not always consistently available. Therefore, the healthy children may eventually become more comfortable with inconsistency than with consistency, and in extreme cases, they are the most comfortable when in "crisis mode." In early adulthood, they may even, although unconsciously, create crises in their own lives in order to return to familiar ground.

Forming Adult Relationships Outside the Family

In dealing with an alcoholic parent or a disabled sibling, one must contend with what would ordinarily be considered inexcusable behavior and must adapt to it. One outcome is an adult who becomes a "doormat," tolerating and excusing inexcusable behavior in all others, whether they be mates, friends, or co-workers. Because the quality of the emotional relationships at home may not be stable, the patterns of these relationships may interfere with the later ability to develop friendships. In some cases, any opportunity to bond with others may be seized and developed too quickly.

Unclear Boundaries

In the case of particularly physically active or low-functioning disabled children, both physical and emotional boundaries are often blurred. In an effort to decrease tension, the parents may appease the disabled child by giving the child what she or he wants, but this appeasement only worsens the other children's feelings of having their boundaries invaded and blurred, although it may accomplish the parent's short-term goal of reclaiming peace and quiet.

Self-Blame

When parents need to rationalize or explain the outbursts or inappropriate behavior of an alcoholic or a disabled child, the healthy siblings may be blamed directly or indirectly for incidents that are clearly not their fault. For example, if a drunk parent trips over a bike, a child may be blamed for leaving her bike around. Similarly, the siblings of an autistic child may be told, "Your brother likes his soap bars in rainbow order and, when you took a bath last night you left them out of order; *that's* why he got upset today.' If this blaming occurs persistently, children will begin to accept it and even to blame *themselves* for events that are clearly not in their control. As an internalized personality trait, this tendency has unfavorable consequences in adulthood and opens one up to abusive relationships.

Fear of Abandonment

Both in alcoholism and with a disabled child in the home, the parents are preoccupied, both emotionally and physically. Their inconsistent availability and insufficient nurturing may cause their children to feel an underlying fear of abandonment. If this fear persists without being worked through, it can cause problems in adult relationships.

Repressing Legitimate Anger

Because in families with handicapped children there is already "difficult behavior" to deal with, anger often has to be repressed so that the rest of the family can function without a constant sense of threat. The expression of anger is often seen as only making matters worse. As a result, anger often goes unresolved or is buried, only to emerge in later outbursts. It's helpful for families to develop avenues for the appropriate expression of anger. (This topic will be discussed in Chapter 10.) Sometimes, this repression of anger extends to matters that have nothing to do with the handicapped sibling.

Keeping It In

Alice Langley, age thirty-three, has a thirty-one-year-old mentally retarded brother. She remembers that when her family made a move to Tennessee, she was twelve years old and very much concerned about losing her friends at home and making new ones in Tennessee. Her mother brushed off these feelings by telling her, "C'mon, you have no problems making friends." What Alice had really needed was just to talk and have her concerns validated. Looking back, Alice wonders whether her mother really believed what she said, or whether her mother simply did not have the energy to deal with Alice's emotions about the move.

Holidays and Family Gatherings

Holidays and family gatherings are often difficult and unpredictable enough when everything is "normal." When an alcoholic or a disabled child is a part of the family, any group gathering may induce anxiety. An alcoholic parent may drink; a disabled child may disrupt. Family dynamics, including parental differences over discipline, are accentuated, and conflict with relatives is also intensified.

Relationships with Relatives

Relationships with relatives are often strained both in families with alcoholics and in families with a disabled child, In both cases, the relatives may feel that their help or helpful suggestions have gone unheeded. Often, parents perceive relatives as being less compassionate and understanding than they should be. The immediate family of the disabled child sometimes feels isolated from the larger family for these reasons. Some of these feelings may be legitimate, and some may be due to oversensitivity. It may be very stressful for parents to try to distinguish those who are truly trying to help from those who, for their own reasons, intrude with destructive opinions. The presence of a disabled child in the family is bound to affect the extended family, either driving people apart or drawing them together.

Feeling Different

Children from a family in which someone is ill may feel different from other children as a result. Children may think that they have the same illness, or that they may catch what the affected sibling has. Sometimes, they will believe that something that they or the affected sibling did caused the problem in the first place. This belief may leave them with the impression that an immense amount depends on their behavior, which is quite a burden for a child.

Maladaptive Coping in Families with a Developmentally Disabled Child

When presented with a stressor, for example, a developmental disability such as autism or alcoholism, a family is thrown out of balance and everyone is likely to be affected. Deliberate steps, professional intervention, patience, and lots of practice are required. Finding help may be more than the parents bargained for and may initially add more stress still. If the outcome is left to chance, the result is often maladaptive coping and a dysfunctional family, the impact of which lasts well beyond childhood. The first step is usually recognition of the problem and recognition of the maladaptive coping and defense mechanisms that may already be operating or that may arise.

Thus far, we have discussed some of the similar consequences of having developmental disabilities and alcoholism in the family. In the remainder of this chapter, we address some of the maladaptive defense mechanisms used in coping. We have included some questions in the appendixes to help identify some of the maladaptive coping styles in your own family.

The Blame Game

Although finger pointing is common in all families, the events that trigger blaming and finger pointing may be different in families with a disabled child. For example, an autistic child may toss a book out the window when he is upset because his brother walked through his line of books, breaking the line. The parents will perceive the movement of the books as the cause of the problem and blame the four-year-old sibling who moved them because he is seen as having more volitional control over the situation. In fact, it is the autistic child's need for order that is at the root of the problem, and what the family may need is help in redirecting the autistic child's desire to line things up so that new tensions over similar incidents won't occur.

Another pattern that often gets the blame game going is parents' blaming each other for everything from carrying bad genes, to not disciplining the child, to disciplining him or her too much. They may even disagree on how severe the child's illness really is, so that communication is difficult and blaming is easy (this topic is discussed in greater detail in Chapter 3). Blaming is never adaptive. Like alcoholism, autism means that one family member's behavior is often unpredictable. It is much easier to blame someone for these disruptions than to accept that they are ultimately under nobody's control. Although it may be difficult to tolerate this realization, in the long run everyone benefits if these situations are seen as unavoidable facts of life with a disabled child. This realization will stop the blame game and will help the family learn to solve problems effectively.

Defense Mechanisms

When faced with any type of life-threatening or life-altering event, the body and mind respond in a number of ways. The function of defense mechanisms in protecting our psyches can be likened to how the body acts to protect itself when one feels threatened. In the case of a physical threat or illness, a number of protective mechanisms may be called into action.

In the classic "fight or flight" response, the body is on red alert, the eyes open wide, the heart beats faster, and the blood flow is drawn away from the surface in order to minimize bleeding in the event of injury. In the case of a broken bone or sprain, swelling protects the area against further injury. In the immediate short run, these reactions have some benefit, but in the long run, these mechanisms do harm; thus, we put ice on an injury to minimize swelling, and we seek medical attention to address the underlying injury and correct it.

The same applies to emotional and mental injury. Having a developmentally disabled child in the family causes not only the emotional trauma of the initial diagnosis but also fatigue from the chronic difficulties and traumas posed by living with this family member. Although the body can handle being on "red alert" occasionally, it would burn out under chronic stress. Emotional equivalents to "swelling" are the classic "defense mechanisms," which function to conceal our initial hurt and protect us from further injury. Like swelling, these defenses provide some initial relief, but if left alone and untreated, the underlying injury will only worsen.

During times of emotional trauma, we often feel disorganized and out of control; this sense of helplessness is very disorienting. Ideally, the best way to regain equilibrium is to address the problem and solve it. This is easier said than done, however, and unless you are a hyperlogical creature like Mr. Spock from "Star Trek," it is something that must be learned and practiced. We can learn by becoming familiar with the defenses that each of us has used in the past, and through self-examination, we can recognize when these defenses have served well and when they have blocked the resolution of conflicts. It may be helpful to look back on your own experience and develop a sense of how you and each of your family members have used these defenses when dealing with painful feelings about your sibling.

Below are some of the common defense mechanisms and how they are often called into play by siblings growing up with developmentally disabled children.

Displacement. Displacement is a means of defending oneself against unpleasant feelings about one thing or person or issue by "displacing" them onto another person or issue. For example, feelings of frustration, anger, or helplessness over a child's diagnosis and limitations may be transferred to other children in the family. Negative feelings that the parent has toward the disabled child may be displaced onto a child who seems to be able to take them better. Through displacement the nondisabled siblings may be made to feel bad as they receive the brunt of the anger intended for someone else. Some siblings experience this displacement as survivor guilt (guilt over having been spared the developmental disability).

Reaction formation.   A reaction formation occurs when any negative feelings are left unprocessed, and instead the opposite sentiment is felt, often in an exaggerated form. For example, feelings of anger toward a child may result in an exaggerated overprotection of the child or something equally selfless, such as an exaggerated involvement in community services.

In families dealing with a developmental disorder, not only is the disappointment not expressed, but an individual may overreact in the opposite direction, that is, with a "reaction formation," and, for example, claiming how much better off the family is for having a disabled child, how fortunate it is to have had this experience, which has brought the family together. To a certain extent, this may be the case, but when asked directly, most people, if given a choice, would not have chosen to have a disabled family member. It is impossible to tell exactly how close these families would be without this additional burden.

Siblings in particular are at risk of developing a reaction formation that may become so all-consuming that they eventually influence major aspects of identity, such as job choice. Disproportionate numbers of the siblings of developmentally disabled children become "helping professionals" such as teachers, doctors, and social workers. This is not bad in and of itself. But for the sake of their own identity formation, it is important for young adults with developmentally disabled siblings to explore whether a career choice is being made for its intrinsic appeal, or to serve a fantasy that they may somehow be able finally to "rescue" their sibling and so resolve feelings of emotional conflict that the sibling's disability has caused.

James Miller, age thirty-three, has a thirty-four-year-old sister, Donna, who has Down's syndrome. Their mother pursued a career in special education. James claims that he felt implicit pressure to go into special education, too, and eventually got his first master's degree in education. He then realized that he didn't enjoy the work at all and, indeed, wanted to make more money. He got his second master's degree in economics and now is much happier pursuing this career. James reports that whenever he expressed anger, frustration, or disappointment, his mother, who was the "master of guilt," would tell him, "Oh, James, I've done so much for you. Don't you know how hard it is? It's been really brutal for me. You're so uncaring. You're so selfish, just like your father."

At a younger age, a sibling may show an exaggerated concern for the disabled child's welfare and may be willing to take on the responsibility for the child (see Chapter 6 on the parentified child). It is perfectly natural for children—even those in families without a disabled member—to feel anger and resentment over how their life is affected by a sibling. To some extent, all siblings need to sublimate angry feelings or convert this energy to a more positive use. And when there is a disabled sibling, family events are often disrupted, there may be frequent outbursts at home and in public, rules seem to revolve around the disabled sibling, and parental time and attention are siphoned off to a great extent by the disabled child. It is the responsibility of the parents to help the nondisabled children feel safe in expressing their feelings; anger can be frightening even to the person feeling it, and children need to be told that such feelings do not mean that they do not "love" their brother and do not make them bad people. Children need to know that feelings are just feelings, and not powerful enough to cause anything bad to happen. So although reaction formation may convert negative energies to positive uses, sometimes just allowing a child to express negative feelings is a more direct way of addressing despair.

Projection. In projection, unpleasant feelings such as anger are projected onto an external source. Often, feelings of frustration over the disabled child's lack of progress are projected onto special-education teachers and the social service agencies responsible for getting services for the child. Rather than directly experiencing the frustration as being related to the child, parents may feel that the schools and other helping agencies are uncaring or are even conniving to deprive them of services they are due. Sadly, as parents act on their projected feelings of anger and frustration, teachers, social workers, and others who experience the parent's feelings may turn off and avoid the family, so that the projection becomes destructive and self-fulfilling. In some families, frustration with the child (say, with her or his tendency to take things that belong to others) is projected onto neighbors or relatives when they mention that they would like to "help Josh understand not to take that bike because it belongs to Melissa." Well-meaning attempts to provide helpful analysis of the child's problems or to intervene directly may be met with anger at the helper.

The siblings of developmentally disabled siblings may also be the recipients of parental projection. Parents may see a nondisabled sibling as having the same traits that the disabled child has and may even perceive the traits as worse, and as more of a problem in the nondisabled child. Sometimes, this happens because it is easier to criticize and try to change the traits in the nonhandicapped child. The normal sibling is seen as having "no excuse," and parental anger that is truly felt about a trait of the disabled child's may be unleashed on a mild version of the trait when it appears in the normal child. Thus, parents may yell at a five-year-old girl for being sloppy when she's left some of her toys out—even though a normal five-year-old can be expected to do such things. A mother of a hyperactive mentally retarded boy may never try to make her mentally retarded child hold still, even though he constantly knocks things over and grabs things that belong to others. But when this mother's other boy so much as runs down the hall on the way to the bathroom, he may be verbally reprimanded for acting too wild.

Regression. In regression, a person "regresses" to an earlier means of coping, becoming dependent on and perhaps demanding of others as a younger child would. In the case of siblings, an older sibling may behave in a way that will demand more attention. Usually, in siblings of developmentally disabled children, these effects are subtle and sometimes even lie outside the child's conscious control. For example, an eight-year-old may develop bed-wetting around the time his four-year-old sibling is diagnosed as needing special education and so much family attention has turned away from him. A younger nondisabled sibling may regress by being exceedingly clinging, trying hard to sit in the mother's lap, especially as a means of excluding the handicapped sibling when he or she is distressed and wants the mother's attention, too.

Intellectualization. Many well-educated families respond to an emotional crisis by creating distance between themselves and the pain by treating the matter as if they were uninvolved third parties. The resulting negative affect may be that the family implements so many rules on how to live with the developmentally disabled child that spontaneity and a sense of individual relationships are destroyed. One limitation of some of the intensive in-home programs that are now being used with autistic children is that parents and siblings are turned into cotherapists and must constantly monitor their interactions with the autistic child, making sure that he or she responds in full sentences, makes eye contact, and so on. Although the practice of such communication skills is very much needed by the child, the child may come to be seen as part of a training exercise and less of a human being.

Acting Out. *Acting out* refers to directing anger indirectly toward a person or institution when to do so directly would be socially unacceptable. Some siblings act out by behaving aggressively toward younger, more helpless children outside the home. In the sibling of a developmentally disabled child, acting out may also take the form of getting into trouble in school and other activities that cause the parents to make special trips to deal with his or her problems, just as they do for the handicapped sibling. In Chapter 8, we talk more about this means of coping.

More Positive Coping

In certain contexts, the idea of a defense mechanism, or *defensiveness*, is seen as maladaptive, whereas the term *coping* is associated with positive adjustment. The defense mechanisms that we have reviewed here both illustrate problems that occur as a result of maladaptive coping and also point out how each defense, in moderation, may serve a positive function in coping. In the next four chapters, we discuss four prototypical styles of coping that are often seen in the siblings of developmentally disabled children. In Chapter 10, we discuss some of the more positive ways of coping with and adapting to having a handicapped child in the family.

Chapter 6

The Parentified Child

If I am not for myself, who is for me? And if I am only for myself, what am I?

HILLEL, a Jewish teacher, C. 30 B.C.E.–9 C.E.

Defining *Parentification*

Parentified child is a term that can be used to describe siblings who react to a disabled brother or sister by precociously taking on a parental or caregiving role with respect to that sibling. The parentified child exemplifies a form of coping that at first glance may appear quite adaptive. After all, what's wrong with a child who is willing to help his or her parents in caring for a child with a handicap? Isn't learning the importance of caring for and making sacrifices for others at an early age a blessing in disguise? It is a widely held value that growing up with a child with a developmental disability will make someone more tolerant and understanding of others, as well as more compassionate. So what is wrong with this picture?

From one perspective, growing up with more responsibilities does indeed imbue one with a greater sense of responsibility, resulting in being a "better" person for having had the experience.

113

This seems to make sense, at least superficially. However, with a closer look, for many siblings the reality isn't always as ideal as it appears. Growing up taking care of someone else may have negative consequences if this tendency is not kept in check.

A great drawback of parentification is the loss of one's own childhood. Emotional and psychological development follow a natural trajectory: At the earliest ages, up to three or four, the child is normally egocentric, or self-centered. Between five and twelve, the latency years, children become quite rule-oriented; knowing rules, making up rules, and obeying rules provide strong guidance for all sorts of behaviors having to do with being "fair," like sharing, turn taking, and competing. After age twelve, with the onset of adolescence, children naturally strive for an identity that is separate from everyone else's. The process of parentification may interfere with each of these stages. In the egocentric preschool years, parentification prematurely pushes children into a more latency-age stage of following rules that are needed to compensate for the difficulties imposed by having a developmentally disabled sibling who herself or himself has lingered too long in the egocentric stage. In the latency years, parentified children are pushed into taking responsibilities like babysitting, a task usually given only to adolescents, who are regarded as having more fully formed capacities for judgment. As adolescents, parentified children are pushed into adulthood, and the normal phase of experimentation with different identities is cut short by the need to take on a specific adult role—that of caregiver, manager, and sometimes teacher—for the developmentally disabled sibling.

The Circumstances of Parentification

Multiple different factors are at play here. A number of central questions need to be asked and answered for each nondisabled sibling in a family. One should take these questions into consideration when a child is observed to be taking on a caregiving role for her or his sibling that is beyond what is expected.

Figure 6.1. This series of five drawings is by an eight-year-old sister, Cindy, of a six-year old autistic brother, Ben. Ben almost never initiates interactions with Cindy and frequently turns away from her constant attempts to engage him. These pictures are Cindy's fantasy of the brother–sister relationship she longs for—one in which she and Ben "find" each other and can engage in mutual loving.

Although it may seem cute and appropriate, sometimes it isn't. When a child appears to be overly parentified, try to take the following questions into consideration:

1. To what extent has the child taken on family-related responsibilities he or she might not have if a sibling were not disabled?
2. Under what conditions were these responsibilities taken? (That is, how much choice did the child have?)
3. Was responsibility gradually shifted onto this child out of convenience or necessity?
4. What has been the parents' response when the child refuses or is reluctant to take on responsibilities?
5. What has been the parents' response when the child has been helpful? Has he or she received praise, or have the efforts been taken for granted?
6. What would be the parents' response if the child complained about the inconveniences of having a disabled sibling in the family?

If a child is taught to help others in need because that is the moral thing to do, the lessons in having a handicapped sibling can indeed become a way to learn altruism. Along with this lesson, however, a child must also learn to listen to his or her own voice, to own his or her own feelings, and not to feel guilty about less than total selflessness. The child needs to know that it is normal and expectable to sometimes feel angry and resentful but still to want to help out.

The danger for nonhandicapped siblings occurs when they are taught either explicitly or implicitly that they must take on a parentified role in order to receive love and approval from their parents and other significant people in their lives. It can be very difficult to unravel the level of coercion in the parentification process. For the adult sibling of a handicapped person, looking back on childhood and accurately attributing one's own parentified behavior to parental coercion, or to rightful parental attempts to teach altruistic behavior, is a very difficult task.

The concept of codependency was discussed in Chapter 5. Many characteristics of siblings who function as codependents are epitomized in parentified children, whose life and feelings revolve around someone else and his or her problems. Further, the concept of codependency highlights how it is possible for codependents (i.e., parentified children) to suppress their own ability to develop a satisfying emotional life beyond activities that center on caring for and interacting with their sibling.

Boiled Frogs and the Process of Parentification

A family's confrontation with the hardships of raising a disabled child is gradual. It unfolds as the child's disability becomes increasingly apparent, and as the disabled child's trajectory of development diverges increasingly from that of his or her peers. The responsibilities doled out to the parentified child are also gradual and therefore seem natural rather than abnormal. This is not unlike the story of the frog, which, if placed suddenly in a pot of boiling water, will jump out but, if left in cool water that is gradually heated up, will remain there and get burned.

The impact and consequences of the roles taken on in childhood are lifelong. The roles are not absolute, however, and there is usually a lot of "gray zone," as roles change with time, especially as the family grows. Although one role may predominate, components of other roles are often present as well; for example, the parentified child may also be a superachiever or may be withdrawn when outside the family. Or if the parentified child is initially an older brother, a younger female sibling may later take on the parentified role instead as the brother enters adolescence and becomes more naturally independent from the family, and the sister enters the latency years where being "moral" is such a prominent drive.

All children seek approval from the adults in their lives, especially their parents. Parentified children easily pick up the subtle signs that tell them that caring for their sibling will gain them the most, if not all, approval from their parents. The parents themselves may not even be aware of or may consciously deny this circumstance. The scenario for the parentified child may proceed as follows: The parents adapt by being drawn closer to the developmentally disabled child (they may do so because he or she needs so much more care). The normal child senses this closeness and, fearing abandonment by the parents, adapts to the sibling (the "primary stressor") in a way that is specific to the effect of the situation on himself or herself: The child draws closer to the sibling, too, in order to be around the parents more, to form an alliance with the parents, and thus to gain their approval. In other words, in order to be allied with the parents, the sibling adopts a parent role, too. Thus, the cycle of adaptation by being parentified is set up.

> "Mack Darling. Are you done? Can you go in there and just"—her voice rose with a frantic edge—"Just keep him away from that stuff till we get there?" . . . "Why do I always have to?" (Sue Miller, *Family Pictures*)

Acting on Behalf of Your Sibling

It is often too easy to expect nondisabled siblings to take on an adult role and act with a maturity beyond their years. They may be expected to be understanding when their parents ask that they do things that are usually not part of the "job description" for being a sibling. A very benign example is cleaning up toys: Under ordinary circumstances, most parents expect each child to clean up his or her own toys when finished playing. Perhaps if the big brother is four and the little sister is one, the four-year-old will be asked to clean up for his sister. But under ordinary circumstances, this happens during a transient period of development. By the time the younger child is three years old or so, the siblings typically accept the fact that each must clean up after herself or himself and will stage bitter territorial battles in front of their parents, with each child claiming that the other is responsible for the disarray and therefore should be the one to complete the cleanup. Parentified siblings not only come to accept that they must often clean up for both but may go out of their way to show that they are the ones cleaning up for both. Often, in our clinic, while we talk to parents, the normal sibling plays quietly near the adult conversation in a small, contained way (like sitting at a table, drawing with markers, and never even looking up), while the disabled child trashes the rest of the playroom—kicking blocks, scattering toy soldiers, and pulling everything he or she can reach off the shelves. Then, at cleanup time the normal sibling obediently does the majority of the pickup, often without prompting and without complaint. These same normal siblings are the proverbial "little pitchers with big ears." Although they appear to be engaged in their own activities, they are often following the adult dialogue closely, as evidenced by the fact that such children will suddenly chime in with a factual correction like "No, Mommy, Paul didn't fall off his bike at Grandma's; he fell off his bike at Auntie Janey's," or "*I* can make him talk and ask for juice!" They see themselves as equal (although frequently silent) partners in the care of their disabled brother or sister.

Subjugating Normal Childhood Desires

Sometimes parentification involves being like a parent in that children are expected to subjugate their personal desires for their "child" just as a parent does. The siblings are expected to be mature enough to understand when family outings and vacations must be disrupted. We have heard many, many stories about abortive trips to Disneyland. (Wouldn't it be nice if Disneyland had a policy of returning money to families who have to leave early because their disabled child can't handle the stimulation— and if they would then give a free admission to the parents and the nonhandicapped siblings, provided they leave the disabled child at home on the second try?) The parentified sibling is often the family's revisionist historian. For example, a recent family came to visit our clinic from the far reaches of northernmost California; they had just come up from Disneyland, stopping to see us on their way back home. (That, in and of itself, says something about the role of the disabled child as the central figure in the family; that is, the family vacation consisted of two things: a trip to Disneyland, and a trip to see a special doctor for the disabled son, Evan.) With the children out of the room, Evan's parents told how difficult all the lines, waiting, and roller coasters had been on Evan. Later, Evan and his seven-year-old sister, Laura, came back into the interview room, and I said; "So, Laura, I heard you all just got back from Disneyland. How was it?" Laura smiles and said that *Evan* really loved it, and that he went in the teacups with her, let her hold his hand, and didn't even cry until he had to get out of the teacups. When asked what *her* favorite part of Disneyland was, Laura smiled shyly, looked reticent, fixed her gaze on her mother, and didn't continue until her mother prompted her to do so. My concern about Laura's overparentification seemed justified. When Laura went out of the room again, I asked her parents if they ever had a chance to do things with Laura that didn't include Evan, and I suggested that they might consider the benefits to Laura of doing just that.

Taking Responsibility for a Sibling's Safety

Another common responsibility of the parentified child is watching out for the disabled sibling when the children are out with peers—in the yard, on the street, or at a playground. They are told, for example, to "keep an eye out for your brother." The burden of responsibility on a sibling is particularly difficult if he or she is the only family member who can run fast enough to catch the disabled sibling when he or she runs away, or the only one strong enough to hold the disabled sibling down if he or she begins to engage in violent behavior. Often, by the time some children with developmental disabilities are young teenagers, their parents can no longer control them physically, and their siblings of about the same age must be relied on to be the "strong arm."

Although even the parents of nonhandicapped children commonly ask older siblings to watch out for younger ones, the situation is more difficult when the sibling being watched is disabled, is older than the child doing the watching, or is exceptionally hard to control. Chances are that a disabled child will be more active, or more unpredictable, and will be less likely to stay a part of the group activity than a nondisabled child. The nonhandicapped sibling is also left with the task of trying to explain to the peer group what is "wrong" with the sister or brother—why she or he walks funny, talks funny, looks funny, and so on. Other kids make remarks in somewhat cruel jest in order to cover their own anxiety and lack of comprehension when in the unaccustomed presence of a disabled person. Often, such comments exact a greater price from the nondisabled sibling than from the disabled one (who may not understand the mean nature of the other children). Any signs of rejection of the disabled sibling by other children will be frightening to the parentified child as well, because they stir the child's own feelings of ambivalence, however deeply buried. Even when the nonhandicapped sibling (or the relevant adults) get the peer group to understand and accept the nature of the disabled child's problem, the disabled child may still be partly excluded because she or he may not be able to keep up with what's going on, and again it falls to the sibling to act as the "parent" and insist to the others that more be done to include her or him. Sometimes, this is so difficult for parentified siblings that they opt to become reclusive, staying home more to play with the disabled sibling themselves, and hanging out with friends less than their peers do, especially if parents insist that the child always take his disabled sibling along when he goes out.

Repression and Expression of Ambivalent Feelings toward the Disabled Child

Despite outward behavior, there may be a lot of internally felt ambivalence toward the disabled sibling. It is anathema to parentified children that they may actually experience feelings of rejection toward the disabled sibling. Nevertheless, negative feelings, however deeply buried, and however taboo to acknowledge out loud, may be a part of the internal psychic world of non-disabled siblings that is often frightening. Some parentified actions may occur in guilty compensation for "bad" thoughts about the disabled brother or sister. Just as it can be difficult for parents to acknowledge how disabled a child may be, the same may be true of the parentified sibling. Parentified siblings may deny the existence of certain of the disabled sibling's symptoms because they may secretly feel that if they only did more to help, those symptoms wouldn't be as much of a problem.

Taking Actions to Understand and Help the Parentified Child

How can parents help a parentified child? It is important for parents to become comfortable with their own feelings, even their ambivalence, toward their disabled child, and to come to terms with these feelings. Only then can they create a safe place for their nondisabled children to feel and express their ambivalence, too. Once these feelings are recognized, true compassion can grow, and the parents can empathize with the extra burdens put on the nondisabled siblings. Until then, the parents tend to show only exaggerated approval of the nondisabled children's caretaking help and cannot acknowledge how large a toll may be exacted in meeting the affected sibling's special needs. Because girls are more encouraged to become the caretakers in the house, they are more likely to become "little mothers," even if they are younger than the disabled sibling. They will be expected to take care of his or her clothes, cook his or her meals, and comfort him or her when he or she is distressed. The boys are likely to become little "body-guards," the protectors. They will be expected to look out for the disabled child outside the home, protecting him or her from physical danger and even from emotional abuse by other children in the neighborhood.

Parents also need to focus on the other aspects of their nondisabled children's lives. They need to show approval and happiness about things that they might take for granted, like doing well in school, winning a Little League game, or just learning something new about life. Because of the pressures that are associated with managing the disabled sibling, the parents may have to formally designate which of them will pay attention to the nondisabled siblings' issues at a particular time (e.g., Mom and Dad may trade off evenings for helping with homework). This strategy can be really helpful if the nondisabled children know clearly which parent is "there" for them and when, and that, during this time, they are the one who can *get* help rather than being the ones to *give* it.

Parentified coping tends to have effects that change with time. If parents make no efforts to deal with parentification, addressing the effects of parentification may remain a therapeutic task for the sibling as he or she enters adulthood and begins to learn what he or she is capable of being like in a loving relationship. If the parentified role is all a child has had positive feedback for, the result may be corresponding adaptations as an adult, so that caretaking of another dependent person is the only kind of gratification that is sought in a loving relationship. At some point, an adult sibling may come to see this pattern as dysfunctional and may have to expend a great deal of mental energy coming to grips with his or her childhood role, and resenting it. Other adult siblings have an easier time and may spontaneously experience adult relationships in which they come to realize that they are valued for traits other than their caretaking ability, so that they have a chance to make smoother transitions into caring adult relationships.

Recognizing the Parentified Child

Sometimes, seeing and identifying the parentified child is not as easy as it may seem. This is true whether you are a parent or an adult sibling. We have listed below some of the characteristics and traits common to parentified children.

Approval Seeking.   In childhood, parentified children exhibit an intense seeking of approval from their parents. Observing such children, one sees the child's many constant, surreptitious glances toward the parent when he or she does something that might be perceived as not quite right. Similarly, every successful interaction that the parentified child had with a disabled sibling is followed up with a quick glance to the parent to see if the good deed has been noted. The more a child does for the disabled sibling, the more praise he or she gets from the parents. This sets up a positive feedback loop, where the praise and the activity potentiate each other. Getting out of such a cycle in order to spend more time doing what other children the same age do can be quite difficult, especially for a child who, in so doing, risks the real possibility of feeling and being abandoned by his or her parents. The parents begin to expect this child to perform caretaking responsibilities, and they may even come to depend on it. This is especially so as the children get older and take on the more demanding roles that the parents themselves might typically perform. This process has important implications for parentified siblings in adolescence and young adulthood, when they are making important life decisions and starting families of their own (e.g., going to an out-of-town college or thinking of relocating because of a job). We discuss this topic in more detail later.

"What, Me Angry?"   Parentified siblings often express little, if any, anger, even when anger is justified. Such children may feel vulnerable because they sometimes experience feelings of abandonment and/or the withdrawal of approval by their parents. Unlike children who receive more unconditional approval from their parents just for being themselves, parentified children's approval is often contingent on specific actions, and ceasing those actions may make them feel that their tenuous parental approval will disappear. Because parentified children receive so much approval for taking on the parentified role, the expression of any anger or resentment toward the sibling (i.e., rejection of the parentified role) is likely to meet with disapproval from the parent. The signs of parental disapproval don't have to be blatant (such as explicitly telling a child that she or he should be ashamed for feeling or acting negatively toward the disabled sibling). They can be as subtle as the parent's ignoring the expression of the nondisabled child's upset feelings provoked by the disabled sibling, or the parent's not validating that these upset feelings are really being experienced. The specter of being abandoned or rejected is perhaps the most frightening possibility in children's lives. Even though this is seldom a real possibility, it is a fear that children often feel on some level, especially if the parents and the family life center on a handicapped child's problems and condition.

Becoming the Miracle Worker.   The parentified child often takes on the role of teacher and therapist. Even when much formal help is being obtained for the disabled child, the parentified child feels the need to be a teacher and helper, too, copying the teaching strategies used by the parents, behavior therapists, or others who come to the home to help. Research has, in fact, shown that other children, rather than adults, *may* be more effective in eliciting language, social, and play skills from some disabled children. A sibling who *is* particularly gifted in getting a brother or sister to learn things runs the risk of being cast in the role of "miracle worker." Some siblings become like Helen Keller's teacher, Annie Sullivan, an admirable role indeed, but not one that should be foisted unwittingly on a child. It is a tremendous responsibility for siblings to feel that they may be the best or only people who can get their brother or sister to respond in a certain desirable way.

Relationships with Other Siblings.   When their feelings are hurt and difficulties arise, it is often the parentified child from whom other nondisabled siblings seek help. Early in childhood, this may mean giving up an afternoon in the playground with other children in order to help the other siblings cope with their anger or hurt feelings. When the mother is emotionally unavailable to her children because she is so wrapped up in the care of her disabled child, a parentified older sister may become the surrogate "mother" for her younger normal siblings, as well as helping out with the disabled sibling. Later, this sister may be the one everyone calls to "dump on," as when the siblings are all older and in college and things aren't going well. If she can't help, she may be the one who is blamed for being unsupportive, rather than the parents, as the other siblings have long ago given up expecting any kind of emotional support from their parents.

Roles may eventually be reversed so that even the parents come to look to this sibling for comfort and emotional nurturance, rather than the other way around. In this case, not only has this child been denied a legitimate carefree childhood, she is also called on as an adult to make sacrifices for the rest of the family. Naturally, this tendency, unchecked, tends to generalize to other relationships outside the family.

Janina Hartman, age thirty-four, is a good example of the phenomenon just described. She has a thirty-nine-year-old autistic brother, Sidney. At her parents' urging, she has pursued a career in psychiatric social work, so that she can be well informed about the best options for caring for Sidney once her parents are no longer able to. Her parents, the Goodmans, in fact are quite elderly, and even though the psychoanalytic explanations for autism went out the window a good twenty years ago, they still feel guilty that their son's disability had been caused, as a psychoanalyst once told them, by the father's conveying a fear of childhood to the boy—because the father himself had a fear-filled childhood as the resident of a concentration camp in Nazi Germany. Conversation with the Goodmans about Sidney consists mainly of requests to write things down so they can be discussed with their social worker daughter. Their visits are followed by calls from Janina to "touch base" on recommendations for Sidney. Janina is everybody's caregiver: Sidney's and her parents'. One hopes there is someone who takes care of her.

Adolescent Backlash

Once parentified children reach adolescence, they may not want to continue a pattern of self-sacrifice and may prefer to strike out on their own—a natural drive that arises in adolescence. Developing an identity separate from one's family is a difficult enough part of growing up under normal conditions, but it may be much more difficult for the parentified child on whom the family has come to depend, and from whom it expects much.

Adolescents may be left with two unhealthy choices. They can either continue to bury their own feelings and desires, or they can make a break, insist on being less "selfless," and start placing some of their own needs ahead of those of others. Unfortunately, the latter choice is often in conflict with the needs of the rest of the family, which has come to depend on these children. Less "selfless" will indeed be seen as more "selfish" by the rest of the family. This new-found urge toward independence, a very healthy instinct, will at best not be encouraged and will at worst be resisted or prevented from occurring.

Parentification versus the Developmental Drive for Independence

As parentified children become young adults, their history of being so depended on for caretaking may impinge on decisions about where to go to college, whether to relocate, and maybe even whom or whether to marry. When parentified children are old enough, the parents will often seek help from them in providing long-term care and responsibility for the sibling (see Chapter 11). Parentified siblings, because of their pseudomaturity, may be called on as confidants or referees in parental marital conflicts as they reach adolescence and young adulthood. The pattern of ignoring one's own needs in favor of those of others is a difficult one to break, especially when others come to depend on and expect this behavior from the parentified child, who, in turn, becomes dependent on the approval and praise that follow such actions.

As young adulthood approaches, the strain of parentification may create a looming barrier as the individual contemplates what it means to be in a marriage or to raise a family. One set of issues revolves around whether the parentified child has a realistic or distorted view of how much responsibility, especially caretaking, is expectable in a marriage or relationship. The parentified child has habitually associated love and familial closeness with caretaking and needs to make very conscious attempts to realize that, in most intimate relationships, one person is not expected to do all the caretaking. The habitual pattern of parentification as a child can cut two ways in an adult: The parentified child, off to school or living on his or her own for the first time, may feel "empty" without someone to care for and may prematurely become involved in a relationship, just to have someone to look after. Such an individual loses the experience of having a period of autonomy and independence in his or her life—a loss that may be regretted in the future. On the other hand, once away from home, the parentified child may have such an intense feeling of relief that the capacity to engage in intimate relationships is impaired because of an unconscious fear of becoming enmeshed in an unrelenting role as a caretaker.

The second set of issues faced by parentified children in adulthood is the possibility of seeking out relationships in which inordinate or actually pathological amounts of caretaking are inherent in the relationship, as in a relationship with an alcoholic, someone with a physical or mental disability, or someone who has a dependent personality and needs a lot of emotional nurturing. As we discussed in Chapter 5, the similarities between the adult children of alcoholics and the adult siblings of the developmentally disabled are close in many ways, and there is often a comfort in staying with what is familiar, even if there is a conscious awareness that what has been familiar is not emotionally healthy.

A third set of issues revolves around the selection of a spouse who may or may not want to share in the long-term responsibilities for the developmentally disabled sibling (responsibilities that the parentified sibling feels he or she must accept). Diana Saunders, age forty-six, is an oncology nurse with a dually diagnosed schizophrenic and mentally retarded younger brother, George. At age forty-three, she was remarried to John. A year later, Diana's mother had a stroke. Her parents lived next door with her retarded brother George, but they were increasingly unable to care for him. George spent more and more time at Diana's house with her and her new husband. They were seen at the point where John, Diana's husband, was insisting that George be put in a residential placement because, according to John, not only did George make intimacy with his new wife impossible, but Diana's teenage children by her first husband were becoming increasingly withdrawn, seldom emerging from their rooms, spending a lot of time out, and never having friends over because they were uncomfortable with the constant presence of their retarded uncle, George. It was just as hard for Diana to see the difficulties that John and her children were experiencing, as it must have been for Diana's parents to have seen the problems they created while raising Diana with the expectation that she should always be George's caretaker.

Who Is at Risk of Becoming a Parentified Child?

Parentification and Birth Order

The birth order is an important influence in determining which coping mechanism a child will adopt, and as we discussed in Chapter 2, older siblings, especially girls, are at the greatest risk of parentification, especially if they are a few years older than the developmentally disabled sibling. It should be noted, however, that we're talking only about probabilities here; there are many exceptions. Nevertheless, the information in this section should help in assessing difficulties within your family or the families that you are caring for.

Firstborn children are most likely to take on the parentified role, but to some extent, this is also true of other older children, who take care of their younger siblings even in the absence of a handicap. One important difference here is that, ordinarily, when older siblings take on the parental role with a younger sibling, the role is temporary. As the younger normal sibling learns more skills and becomes more independent, the responsibilities of the older child ease. This is not the case with a developmentally disabled sibling. The older sibling's responsibilities may increase and may indeed become more demanding with time. Taking care of simple needs like tying shoes or explaining awkward behavior to strangers is more difficult as the developmentally disabled sibling ages. In fact, the parents may rely exclusively on the siblings for certain aspects of caretaking as the developmentally disabled child grows up. For example, a single parent mother will have to rely on her son to take her retarded boy to a public restroom after a certain age. A stronger, older sibling may be depended upon for providing physical restraint during violent tantrums or episodes of self-injurious behavior.

Chronologically, younger siblings are in the awkward position of becoming the "older" siblings as their development exceeds that of their developmentally disabled sibling. Along with the usual burdens of a parentified role, there is also the "embarrassment factor" of a younger sibling doting on an older sibling. The larger the gap in age, the more difficult and awkward this situation will be. A fifteen-year-old girl holding hands in public with a twenty-three-year-old brother who is making weird noises and flapping his other hand is a strange sight. If the older developmentally disabled sibling is at least somewhat aware of this disparity, there may be even more difficulties. The developmentally disabled child may feel unduly rejected and depressed. If a twenty-three-year-old has a mental age of four, he feels as badly about no one's wanting to hold his hand as any four-year-old would. When a younger sibling takes on the parentified role, he or she assumes the role of the firstborn, even if the disabled sibling is really the firstborn.

Parentification and Gender

In most traditional cultures (e.g., Latino, Chinese, and Middle Eastern), child rearing is seen primarily as a woman's role, as was discussed in Chapter 3. Because taking care of a handicapped sibling is essentially a "mother's role," it is usually the girls in the family who are given the nod when it comes to caring for the disabled sibling. For this reason, girls are at the greatest risk of becoming parentified, as was discussed in Chapter 2. This phenomenon is not limited to the cultures mentioned above; it is also true in U.S. culture in the 1990s.

Parentification and the Influence of Family Size

In a larger family, the responsibilities tend to be spread over the entire family and rarely fall to one person. This situation decreases but does not eliminate the risk that any one child will take on the parentified role. It is still something to look out for. In a larger family, the parents have an opportunity to establish a positive pattern early by dividing up the responsibilities more evenly, thus preventing one sibling's having to take on the lion's share. Outings are easier as well in larger families, as the disabled sibling doesn't necessarily stand out as much, and various family members can take turns watching her or him. When parents become elderly, brothers and sisters in a large family can share the care of the disabled sibling so that the burden of care doesn't fall on just one brother or sister. This is particularly important to some families, especially where out-of-home care would be seen as an abdication of family responsibility. Many developmentally disabled children now have normal or near-normal life spans because of surgeries that correct congenital defects and medications that treat recurrent health problems, and so these individuals will need care for a very long time.

Approaches to Coping

Not all of the consequences of parentification are negative. Although we have focused, so far, on the risks, there may be benefits, too, and for some individuals more than others.

Altruism

Taking care of someone early in life may have lasting effects on sensitizing one to the needs of others. Growing up parentified may increase the tendency to be a giving person and to become involved in charitable and altruistic endeavors. Altruism is admirable unless it is performed to the point where one is making unreasonable sacrifices in one's own life. Altruistic behavior may also be motivated mainly by a need for the praise or admiration of others rather than by any real sense of self-satisfaction or increase in feelings of self-worth. When one is an adult, acceptance and love may not always be forthcoming, even following generous acts in situations where one is taking care of an emotionally dysfunctional partner. The parentified child must first learn to care for and love himself or herself and must realize that taking care of oneself is not a form of selfishness. (We are reminded of the instructions on the airlines before takeoff: In the event of an emergency, those traveling with small children are asked to place the oxygen mask on themselves first before placing it on a child. This is a wonderful metaphor for those who grew up as parentified children and need reminders to care for themselves before undertaking the care of others.)

Signs of altruism outside the family may be apparent at an early age. Linda and Ronald Cane, the parents of ten-year-old Ashley, who has multiple physical and cognitive handicaps, told about Ashley's experience of being fully mainstreamed in second grade. When asked if Ashley had made friends, Ron and Linda said with surprise in their voices, "It's so interesting, Ashley's best friend is Lawrence—and he has a two-year-old sister with Down's syndrome!"

A similar experience is of children who volunteer afternoons and Saturdays to be the "nonhandicapped peers" in integrated play and socialization therapy groups run for developmentally disabled children. An examination of the roster of the "nonhandicapped peers" usually shows quite a few who have disabled siblings themselves, or who have parents involved in special education. To some extent, this altruism may be expected because of the way the children are recruited to help out; the leaders of such groups report that these children often participate because their parents feel it "would be good for them." Certainly, such behavior is altruistic, but it is just one choice among the many forms of altruism that parents might encourage in a child that age, like selling cookies to raise money for the Girl Scouts, cleaning up a park or beach with a school class, or singing Christmas carols at a nursing home. Encouraging altruism to handicapped children is what sociologists would call *anticipatory socialization*, that is, early experience with roles that are valued in adults.

Professions such as child social work, pediatrics, child psychiatry, pediatric nursing, child psychology, and especially special education appear to attract disproportionate numbers of individuals who grew up in a family with a disabled child. Although there do not appear to be any formal statistics on the exact numbers, most people in such fields have many colleagues who will list a disabled brother or sister as one justification of their career choice. Parentified siblings tend to go into these fields for a variety of reasons, not the least of which is that they have had years of training and preparation for this role before they ever went to college; it "feels right." The question that should be asked when an adult sibling enters a "helping" profession is: What is the motivation? Is it to receive additional praise? Is it guilt? One also needs to look at how involved a parentified sibling becomes with his or her work. Parentified siblings who grew up with an all-consuming passion to please their parents may, as adults, be "workaholics" with an all-consuming passion to do more and more—to the exclusion of other life goals such as attending to a family of their own.

If adults who were parentified children enter the helping professions in order to receive approval and love, this may not be a sufficient reason. They may risk disappointment when they don't receive the expected "strokes" for having made such a sacrifice. However, if this choice is freely made after a consideration of other options, and no family coercion is involved, this choice may be a wonderful blessing for both the professional and those he or she serves. In any case, a career choice is a difficult life decision. Under normal circumstances, it is a blend of both aptitude and experience. We feel that it is more important than usual for the siblings of developmentally disabled individuals to consider whether they are making a career choice because of aptitude, or because experience has led them to feel that there really is no other good choice.

Once parentified siblings have taken on the role of helping professional, they may enjoy feeling mastery, and feeling superior and more knowledgeable, having professionally lived through many of the problems that were originally personal ones.

Friendships as an Adult

We have mentioned that parentified children often become the "teacher" or "therapist" in the family even before assuming such a role formally as an adult. We feel that problems may arise later in life if the individual's primary identity in adulthood is basically the same as his or her main source of gratification in childhood. In these cases, there is the highest risk that a well-rounded personality will not fully develop, and that the individual will become unidimensional, not seeking gratification from other sources. Such individuals may sell themselves short, abdicating their opportunity to develop other talents and strengths.

However, adults who have survived parentification and have come to understand that their childhood is in the past may be left with some clear benefits. We have already discussed the development of altruism. Another strength may be having developed a good ear for problems and an ability to listen—assets in being a good friend. The key to good adult adjustment for the parentified child lies in how fully the adult can reflect on the experiences of growing up parentified, take inventory of the traits accrued from the experience, keep what is adaptive, and consciously try to work through what is maladaptive.

Chapter 7

The Withdrawn Child

Who Is the Withdrawn Child?

Unlike the parentified child, the withdrawn child copes by removing himself or herself from family activities that increase the stress of having a developmentally disabled child in the family. The parentified child externalizes his or her anxiety. The withdrawn child internalizes it.

Withdrawn children may not really be causing any problems that require anyone's immediate attention, and so their problems in adjusting may go unnoticed. The parents and the other siblings may already be so wrapped up in the problems of the handicapped child that being withdrawn may not seem to be much of a maladaptation. Parentified children make themselves a very functional part of their family by becoming overinvolved in the care of the disabled child. Withdrawn children blend in by becoming almost invisible: "out of sight, and out of mind."

With parents and other family already stretched to the limit, nondemanding, withdrawn children may even be experienced as a welcome relief. Their parents may think or even express themselves along the following lines: "Oh, Grace is the perfect little child; she never gives me any trouble. She just keeps herself busy and doesn't get in the way—such a little angel." Whereas parentified children actively seek parental approval by doing good things and by caring for the disabled sibling, withdrawn children make many fewer efforts to gain parental attention—in the form of either approval or disapproval. It is developmentally normal for children up through the latency years to seek frequent parental attention and acknowledgment. Although a child who does not seek attention may be easy to care for, it is a worrisome thing, and the picture beneath the surface may not be so rosy.

Unfortunately, the withdrawn child often receives lots of praise and positive feedback for staying out of the way, and so withdrawn behavior may be socially reinforced. Overwhelmed parents often send out messages that they don't have the resources to give this child attention. Children easily pick up on these messages, especially when a really frazzled parent accelerates the intensity of his or her "not now, dear" message. On many occasions, I've seen siblings bring parents a toy or picture they've drawn while I've been talking to the parents about the disabled sibling. The parents who encourage withdrawal may at first gently hand back a child's drawing without comment. If the child persists and hands the drawing to the parent again, the parent may give it a cursory look and say, "Not now, dear." The child who initiates this attention seeking yet again usually gets a disapproving stare and an explicit warning to go away and find something else to do. Although the child usually looks at least a little crushed, few cry, and most slink off somewhere and do find something else to do.

Some parents who come to our clinic are even more direct. They'll give a five-year-old a "Go busy yourself!" or a "Don't bother me!" and then be able to successfully forget that a sibling who is six feet away is even present for the next two hours. These are not generally abusive or neglectful parents who in other ways reveal a lack of ability or judgment in parenting. However, such a direct and rejecting parent–child interaction is the result of many similar episodes from which the normal sibling has learned to read the parents' voice, gestures, and words, which convey, "When I say vanish, *vanish.*" The child is complying with parental

Figure 7.1. Maren, age seven, idealizes and integrates her four-and-a-half-year-old brother, Alec, into her family. Although Alec is quite active and has mental retardation, which causes numerous challenges to everyday living, this is portrayed only by the fact that Alec is the one up front, arms outstretched, pushing Maren herself somewhat into the background. Maren is struggling to integrate her idealized family (typically drawn repeatedly by children of this age) and her actual situation.

wishes. Parents who have frequently been overwhelmed by their developmentally disabled child may enforce the withdrawal of normal siblings mainly as a means of triaging who needs their help the most.

Some withdrawn children appear to be part of the action but are present only physically and not emotionally. Six-year-old Justin was building a ramp for Matchbox cars when his two-and-a-half-year-old mentally retarded sister, Betty, came bursting onto the scene. She wrecked the ramp kicking it with her foot, unintentionally, and then, for no apparent reason, proceeded to slap her brother, quite hard, on the nose with her open hand. Justin simply did not react. Although obviously physically present, Justin was emotionally detached from the situation. Earlier, I had been trying to draw Justin out by chatting with him about school, friends, and favorite activities. Once he had established that I seemed interested in him (as well as his sister), he had volunteered in a quite neutral tone of voice that Betty often slapped his face. It was one of those *non sequitur* statements that children of that age sometimes make, but I was struck by Justin's matter-of-fact tone. It was all the more striking that Justin looked neither to his parents nor to me when Betty hit him. Justin's response was what has sometimes been termed *learned helplessness*. He had learned that it made no difference whether he tried to react or not, because Betty's behavior continued despite his own actions.

In other children, withdrawal is a more active behavior that involves active avoidance. The example that follows also illustrates how early reactive patterns to developmentally disabled siblings can begin: Robert, an eighteen-month-old baby brother of a four-year-old autistic boy, Selwin, is the case in point. While Selwin was out of the room, Robert began to eat a cookie his mother had given him. When Selwin returned, he immediately grabbed his brother's cookie and ran. Their mom gave Robert another cookie. When Selwin finished his brother's first cookie, he approached Robert to obtain a second. Robert dodged a few times and used as much strategy and motor coordination as his little eighteen-month-old being could muster. As Selwin lunged, Robert dropped the second cookie and ran. For the next half hour, this same pattern continued, with Robert warily keeping an eye on Selwin as he tried to eat, but withdrawing and dropping his food whenever his brother got too close.

Withdrawn children keep to themselves in their own room and can be left to their own devices for entertainment and stimulation. They exclude others by choice or as the result of being chronically ignored. They may demand very little from their parents because, as noted above, experience or intuition tells them that very little is available. As the cycle continues, they may seek attention less often and may continue to get very little, and so the cycle will intensify and persist.

Even if the parents sense that something is wrong with the withdrawn child, they may not draw the child out precisely because the child provides the necessary respite from the overwhelming task of caring for the disabled child. The parents may notice that something is wrong, but they may rationalize it by claiming that the child is just naturally shy, or a natural bookworm, and so on. Opportunities to counteract withdrawal—for example, by initiating a special activity just for that child—seldom occur because the child does not demand them.

The Roots of Withdrawn Behavior

The parents may come to expect withdrawn behavior from a child and begin to take it for granted. Any deviation from this pattern, or any movement toward emerging from the withdrawn state, may be misinterpreted as "acting out."

It may be easy for withdrawn children to get boxed in by their own behavior. If the usually withdrawn child does reach out for attention, the additional demand on the parents may provide a reaction like "I already have enough problems with your brother without you starting in also." As a result, the withdrawn child may be subjected to even stricter discipline and may be expected to behave more maturely than is reasonable, given his or her age. Although this withdrawn behavior may be convenient and may even seem "all right" at first, it is not without consequence. This child is learning early to internalize her or his difficulties, and not to express emotions.

In some instances, it may be appropriate for the parents to encourage a withdrawn child's limited involvement in the care of his or her sibling. This tactic may be a good start, if it is done with the goal of allowing the withdrawn child to feel more like a full-fledged member of the family. Balance is the key. Drawing the child into some of the caretaking role may be a good way to draw him or her into conversation. The next step would be for the parents to get involved with this child in activities that don't involve the disabled sibling. A great deal of sensitivity is needed to draw a withdrawn child out without making that child into a parentified sibling, too. Change often comes gradually; recognition and patience are crucial, although they are often in short supply in a household with a disabled child.

It is also worth noting that just as a withdrawn child may become a parentified child if caretaking roles are the only ones he or she is encouraged to engage in, it is also possible for the parentified child to become withdrawn. A parentified child who can no longer cope with caregiving demands may simply withdraw. This reaction is particularly likely when the disabled child becomes aggressive toward the sibling, scratching, hitting, biting, or kicking, and making the nondisabled sibling very wary of him or her. Parents need to be vigilant in looking for these and other potential changes over time and should not underestimate how unpleasant it may be for the nonhandicapped child to be attacked by a sibling when resolution through retaliation or negotiation is not possible.

Helping the Withdrawn Child to Feel Better

So far, we have emphasized that withdrawn children become withdrawn because they are responding to a parental desire for them to withdraw. This happens when parental demands for the child to "disappear" occur too often. How is this situation best addressed?

There are certainly times when parents legitimately need to have their children out of sight and out of mind. To achieve a balance, parents need opportunities to do a variety of things without their handicapped child. The parents must be willing to spend time alone together, or with friends, or to take advantage of available respite care so that time to recuperate is built into their lives. If parents can learn to take time away from the handicapped child without feeling guilty, they then have a better chance of focusing some energy on engaging the withdrawn child. A child who responds to stress by withdrawing is vulnerable in specific ways. Such children need parents who are willing to come to them on their own terms—such as doing a joint activity that is of their choosing. Something as simple as having a "sacred" time on Saturday to go with Dad to get ice cream or having Dad coach the child's soccer team can make an enormous amount of difference.

When given a chance to interact, parents should be careful to note whether or not the usually withdrawn child becomes more interested and engaged, or whether he or she is still withdrawn, rejecting overtures, and preferring to be alone. Some children respond to a small amount of direct attention, but it may be much more difficult for others, especially children with a vulnerability to depression, to come around. It may take time for a strategy such as one-on-one outings to build up enough trust and security so that they begin to seem like a good opportunity to really talk, and to allow even the more depressed children to gradually open up.

If a withdrawn child's pattern of isolation seems to become more entrenched over time, it may be really helpful for the child to receive individual therapy. Therapy will provide the child with a special relationship that is just for him or her, and an hour during which all adult attention focuses on activities that he or she initiates. Even if the therapist does not specifically press the child into discussing the withdrawn behavior, the behavior may get better as the child realizes that his or her activities seem fun and interesting to an adult. As self-esteem improves, withdrawal often lessens.

Difficulties Encountered at Home by the Withdrawn Child

The characteristics of those children who are coping by withdrawal change as they develop. We will look in depth at how these people appear as children and what the potential outlook is for them as adolescents and as adults. If you are an adult sibling "looking back," you may recognize yourself and gain some understanding of your coping style both then and also now, as an adult. If you are a parent or a clinician taking care of such a family, this discussion will give you some insight into the existing family dynamics.

Physical Isolation

The withdrawn child tends to seek out an isolated space in the house. In the beginning, the retreat to this space may occur only during family conflicts and difficulties. After a while, the retreat to this spot or another may be constant. In one family we assessed, a twelve-year-old sister from a family of five, with two retarded brothers, had dragged a mattress into the basement and, along with several blankets, had built a "reading fort."

The withdrawn child may develop a tendency to disappear when company arrives. The social stress of behaving in an outgoing fashion may be too much for a child who has developed a habitual pattern of aloneness. Eventually, such a child may not show an interest in interacting with others and may even begin to fail to respond when spoken to.

Compensating with a Rich Fantasy Life

Because withdrawn children are frequently socially isolated, they often have a rich fantasy life, talking to dolls or writing stories and drawing pictures that describe fantasies, sometimes of idealized versions of family life. The fantasy life serves as an idealized world where these children can restore their sense of having more control over things, and perhaps of being more valued (like imagining they are the rulers of a make-believe kingdom and everyone must do what they want). A boy may have fantasies of being a warrior, being aggressive at will. For him, this may help compensate for the unusually strong check on aggression that he must exercise when playing with a physically fragile sibling who may be nonambulatory or may have cerebral palsy. Fantasies about being strong or smart may also help children ward off fears that, someday, they themselves may end up weak or noncomprehending like their affected sibling.

Parents should begin by showing an interest in withdrawn children's fantasy activities, not only as a means of increased interaction with the children, but also as a way of gaining some insight into what they are thinking and feeling. Trying to get withdrawn children to include their mother or father in the play, while allowing them to remain in control of the progress of the imaginary events, is a way to build rapport. Children's fantasy life often serves as a window on their real concerns and thoughts. Paying attention to such activities, therefore, serves three purposes: (1) it draws these children out and makes them feel safer with their parents and the rest of the family; (2) it allows the parents an opportunity to engage in an activity with these children that does not center on the handicapped child; and (3) it gives some insight into what may be genuinely bothering these children. It is a golden opportunity to build trust and a friendship that may define the metaphors through which parents and children may be able to communicate for a long time to come.

In a drawing by the sibling of an autistic boy, the family stands outdoors next to the car, while the autistic sibling, inside, looks out the window. The parents of the child who drew that picture might have asked what was happening in the picture. It would have provided an ideal opportunity for a parent to say, "Yes, it *would* be nice to go on a trip with just you girls and let your brother stay home. If we did that, where would you like to go?" Instead, many parents are afraid that an open discussion of such a picture may open the emotional floodgates, and they quickly squelch emotion, for example, by saying, "Oh, we would *never* go anywhere without your brother. Don't worry!" If a child expresses some feelings through the characters in a fantasy, parents should be responsive and let the child know that his or her feelings are valid, and even that the parent, too, may share those feelings at times.

Being withdrawn into fantasy does not necessarily mean that the child does not care about her or his affected sibling. Thinking about the sibling may simply be painful or overwhelming and fearful. For example, a parent may discover that an unaffected child is fantasizing that a cure for his or her sibling might be found during a visit to the doctor. It's good for parents to check periodically with siblings and gauge what they do and don't understand about the nature of their sibling's disability. Especially scary to young siblings may be the fear that they may "catch" cerebral palsy, epilepsy, or some other strange-looking symptom that only the sibling has. Another common fear is that the siblings themselves may have done something to cause their sister's or brother's disorder or to make it worse.

Escaping through Withdrawal

Talking and engaging with others is difficult enough for a withdrawn and/or shy child; it is even more difficult to talk about very personal issues in one's own life. By withdrawing, a child may be trying to escape reality and/or responsibility. Some nonaffected children may choose not even to count the affected sibling when asked, "How many brothers and sisters do you have?" To mention him or her may obligate a sibling to disclose something personal before being ready to do so; not counting the affected sibling may simply avoid the issue. Parents need to be understanding of such things and to realize that a child does not have the presence of mind to handle such a situation in the same way that an adult does. Instead, writing a disabled child out of a family script may be a way of compartmentalizing the grief and discomfort that thinking about the disabled sibling elicits in some of her or his brothers and sisters in certain settings.

Characteristics of the Withdrawn Child in Adolescence and Adulthood

During intimate relationships and at other times in life when conflicts and disagreements are inevitable, people who were withdrawn as children may be more likely simply to withdraw again, instead of staying with a problem and working out compromises. They are also unlikely to stand up for themselves. They may avoid intimate relationships or end up as passive "doormats" for others. An adult sibling who as a child dealt with family stress by withdrawing may, as an adult, appear stoic and unperturbed by stressors when actually she or he is blocking out the stressful circumstances and not coping with them at all.

There are, however, some positive outcomes of coping through withdrawal. A person who was able to gain release through fantasy and other creative outlets may find them helpful later in life, when spending time alone is appropriate or necessary. Increased capacities for focus and/or creativity may result. These can be both functional and productive.

A learned pattern of withdrawal in response to stress or conflict may lead to an adult life characterized by increased social isolation and avoidance of dealing with difficult issues. In extreme cases, especially when withdrawal is coupled with signs of depression, adult siblings may be at a higher risk of the more severe emotional disorders, as a result of chronically internalizing conflict and anxiety. In particular, withdrawn children are most at risk for depression, alcoholism (and other addictions), anorexia, and a variety of psychosomatic disorders (such as ulcers, cancer, and heart disease).

Who Is at Risk of Becoming a Withdrawn Child?

The sibling who is at risk of developing maladaptive coping through withdrawal may be predisposed to do so by the presence of any of several factors. These factors are both external to the child, such as those relating to family structure, which have already been discussed generally in Chapter 3, and intrinsic to the individual's temperament and personality predispositions.

Birth Order

In families with a developmentally disabled child, the younger and middle children are more often the quietest, tending to blend into the background. (As pointed out earlier, the older ones are more likely to externalize their anxiety by becoming parentified or, as we will see in Chapter 8, sometimes by acting out.)

Children born right after the disabled child may feel parental pressure to perform and to stand out to show that they are not only "normal" but somehow above average in order to help "average out" the family IQ. Understandably, many parents feel deficient on some level after giving birth to a disabled child and may look to subsequently born children to make up the difference, and to assure them that the disabled child was a one-time aberration. Some children have the intellectual capacity and personalities to live up to the extra demands that their parents may place on them. For others, the additional pressure may be too much emotionally or intellectually, and the child may respond by withdrawing.

Children who are chronologically younger but developmentally older than the affected sibling may be seen as growing up in need of no real help. Therefore, they are often left alone. A five-year-old who can tie her own shoes when her ten-year-old brother can't will get little to no help in getting dressed. And if that five-year-old can also read simple books to herself and her brother can't, the brother will be read to more, and she'll probably be read to less. Although the five-year-old may be seen as accomplished and independent, it is important for her parents to realize that most five-year-olds like "help" (admiration) when dressing themselves and still like to be read to, even if they can read simple things for themselves. If this sort of situation describes your family or a family you are caring for, you should realize that such a child may be at risk of becoming more withdrawn over time, as "independence" may translate into self-isolation.

Gender

Girls tend to withdraw more often than boys, as they are more often apt to internalize stress and boys are more likely to externalize stress. Especially when a girl is several years younger than the handicapped child, or if there is an older sibling, she is less likely to be enlisted as a coparent. Girls in particular are at risk of being asked to cope by withdrawing, such as being constantly encouraged to "keep quiet" or "play by yourself" when the parents are preoccupied with the disabled child. Boys who withdraw may be boys who are particularly susceptible to depression.

Detecting Depression in the Withdrawn Child

Siblings of all chronically ill children are at greater risk of depression than the general population. Withdrawal from family life may be a coping strategy. Although withdrawal can have positive and negative aspects, as we've discussed, withdrawal is *not* synonymous with depression. For example, we discussed withdrawn children who engage in very active fantasy lives. However, if a child's habitual method of coping with family stress is to withdraw, it is important to look for emerging signs of depression, too.

Does the child's withdrawn attitude extend beyond settings where the disabled sibling is monopolizing family activity? Does the withdrawn attitude extend to one-on-one interactions with parents or other relatives? One of the key differences between an "unhappy" or "moody" child and a depressed child is the *duration* of the sadness and moodiness. Therefore, it is best to obtain input from several sources (e.g., teachers, relatives, and friends) and to do so over time, to get a clear sense of how long a possible depression has been present. Getting feedback from several sources such as close friends, relatives, or someone from church is particularly important because it is very difficult for parents and those very close to the child to remain objective, or to see the subtle changes that occur over time.

Depression has more often been seen as an adult problem by the medical community and the lay public. Although it does indeed occur in children, it often doesn't "look" the same as it does in adults. Children very rarely, if ever, say, "You know I'm really feeling depressed (or blue, or down) these days." Childhood depression is most often quite preventable or treatable in its initial stages. However, early signs should not be taken lightly or brushed aside as moodiness, or as "a phase" that a child is going through. Given the high risk of childhood depression in the siblings of developmentally disabled children, parents and health care workers need to be vigilant and cognizant of this possibility.

Multiple Risk Factors in Depression

If a child is quiet and shy to begin with and tends to withdraw as a means of coping, his or her ability to establish relationships, so crucial to normal growth and development, may be compromised when others have fewer opportunities to reach out to him or her. Thus, depression may begin as an interaction between preexisting personality traits and nonoptimal family circumstances. A history of major depressions on either side of the family adds to the likelihood that siblings exposed to a strong family stressor like a disabled child will respond with feelings of withdrawal, despondency, and helplessness that may eventually lead to a full-blown depression. Personality, family circumstances like marital discord or divorce, and family history contribute to an array of factors that may increase the predisposition to later depression. The predisposing factors include lower self-esteem, feelings of helplessness, and feelings of being different from one's peers.

Depression Defined

One definition of depression is that it is a reaction to a loss, of a person, a thing, or a state of well-being. Depression is also often accompanied by feelings of helplessness and diminished self-esteem. Certainly these criteria often apply to the sibling of a child with a disability. Helplessness prevails, and the risk of diminished self-esteem is high. Several specific signs of depression are usually investigated when there is a suspicion that a child is depressed.

Anhedonia.   Anhedonia is not only the absence of pleasure or fun in the child's life, but the *lack of a desire* for pleasure and fun. A child who did have fun at one point may stop seeking out friends and may become increasingly withdrawn. A child who does not engage in some mischief and misbehavior may be a welcome relief for an overwhelmed set of parents, but engaging in fun and carefree play is how children should be learning and growing.

Poor School Performance.   Over time, a child who is becoming depressed may show less interest in friends, and his or her school performance may begin to drop off. Teachers may comment that the child doesn't participate much in class and doesn't seem to mind being excluded from social groups during nonwork activities. Depressed or withdrawn children are often preoccupied and distracted by inner thoughts. They may have a difficult time concentrating, and this difficulty often has a detrimental effect on academic performance.

Decreased Energy Level.   A decreased energy level is often manifested as taking naps in the afternoon and declining activities that children normally engage in. Depressed children may also carry themselves poorly and sit in slumped positions. They lack the normal high energy level seen in most children. The depressed child may have frequent psychosomatic complaints, such as headaches and stomachaches, or may complain of feeling too sleepy to do his or her work in school. Depressed children also tend to be less verbal. It can therefore be difficult to obtain information from them, and they may deny feelings of depression, and particularly sad feelings that are in any way tied to their handicapped sibling and how he or she affects life in the home.

Lowered Self-Esteem. Loss of self-esteem leaves one vulnerable to depression. There are many potential sources for lowered self-esteem in connection with having a disabled sibling: (1) if a child identifies with the sibling and has a poor understanding of the disease, he or she may feel (even if unconsciously) also handicapped or flawed in some way; (2) social isolation may leave someone depressed, and siblings who are embarrassed to bring friends home or to interact with neighborhood kids in a park or playground because they are with their handicapped siblings may feel isolated; and (3) low self-esteem may also derive from feeling that one is not meeting parental and familial expectations (whether or not it is really true). When asked to describe themselves, depressed children often do so in the negative. They will state what they are *not*, rather than what they *are* (e.g., "I'm not very good at sports," or "I don't have a lot of friends").

Feelings of Helplessness. For the teenager in particular, the feeling of personal control over one's destiny is very important. When there is a disabled sibling in the family, one's fate is often tied to that of the rest of the family. There may be fewer opportunities to decide what to do or to do things on one's own. This lack conflicts with the adolescent's need for independence and self-determination.

Excessive Guilt. Excessive guilt may be felt by the withdrawn child. If the child is not communicative to begin with, it may be hard to determine if he or she is indeed feeling excessive guilt or not. He or she may feel partially to blame for the problems encountered in the family. If this possibility exists, it should be explored.

Social Isolation and Feeling Different. Identifying oneself as different from one's peers can itself lead to depression, especially in adolescence. Adolescents are exquisitely norm-conscious. Deviance to an adolescent can consist of wearing last year's style of running shoes or tucking in one's shirttails when other guys leave theirs hanging out. Parents who exert pressure on an adolescent to take a disabled sibling along to the movies or out for pizza with friends are probably making a mistake. Although the adolescent may comply, he or she is likely to pay some cost in the peer group and consequently feel different in some way—even if his or her peers are quite supportive. Depressed adolescents may handle the dilemma of contradictory peer and parental expectations by claiming that their peers do not want to get together with them when, in reality, it is they who choose not to put themselves in an awkward situation.

Psychiatric Risk Factors

Children of parents who are depressed or who have other psychiatric illnesses are at greater risk of depression. Because the parents of disabled children are at an increased risk of depression as well as other stress-related disorders, the unaffected children are also at increased risk of depression. Studies suggest that parents will initially feel depressed at the time of the diagnosis. This depression usually resolves itself within the first few years. Other stress-related disorders seem to take longer to develop and may appear in later years, although this subject has not been well-studied. Children with psychiatrically affected parents *are* at increased risk themselves of developing psychiatric symptoms, especially if a parent has been strongly symptomatic (i.e., emotionally unavailable) in the first years of the child's life.

Siblings of developmentally disabled children are certainly at significant risk of depression, and many of the behaviors exhibited by withdrawn children are also some of the behaviors exhibited in depression. Parents are often *not* the first to realize that their child is depressed, especially if the child's withdrawn state serves a positive purpose in family functioning. More often, depression is first suspected by a teacher, a relative, or someone else who cares about the child and knows him or her well. It may be difficult for parents to see depression because the suggestion of a problem in a nonhandicapped child may really make them feel that their parenting skills are being called into question. To acknowledge that yet another child is having problems may carry implications that it is somehow their parenting ability that has caused *all* of the problems.

Professional Help for a Withdrawn, Depressed Child

At first, parents may become defensive when confronted with the possibility that their nonhandicapped child is depressed. Parents in this position need to be given support and understanding. The importance of getting help for the depressed child must be emphasized. Earlier, we discussed how supportive psychotherapy may help withdrawn children develop a better sense of their own unique value and the benefits of greater expressiveness of emotion. In some cases, individual therapy for depressed children may not be enough. A family systems approach may be preferable because the circumstances causing and maintaining the child's depression and withdrawal are part of a complex network of family interrelationships. Therapy is a stressful experience, too, however, and requiring overburdened parents to participate in therapy when they really do not want to be there may not be the best idea. If a therapist has a choice between getting a depressed child from a family with a disabled child into treatment without collateral family visits or not doing therapy at all, the former is probably the better alternative.

Conclusions

So far, we have delineated two major forms of coping and adaptation manifested by the siblings of developmentally disabled children. We have discussed parentified children and with-drawn and depressed children. Next, we will discuss children who respond to the stress of living with a disabled sibling by acting out their feelings of hostility and resentment of the situation on other family members.

Chapter 8

The Acting-Out Child

Acting out is a term used to describe behavior in which an individual *acts out* feelings of anger or hostility, either directly or in a context that engenders the same emotions as the original source of anger. For example, a child who is described as "acting out" in school may be behaving in a challenging and disobedient fashion to a male teacher, in lieu of behaving that way to a controlling, physically abusive father at home, whom he or she fears.

In the context of studying children with developmentally disabled siblings, an acting-out normal sibling is one who acts out negative feelings engendered by the disabled sibling (or by family members acting in that sibling's interests). Like the parentified child, the acting-out child externalizes anxiety and negative affect in an attempt to cope but does so in less socially acceptable ways than a parentified child. Acting-out children draw attention to themselves, but in a negative way, so that their parents and other significant people in their lives are forced to pay more attention to them. Their parents may see the acting-out behavior as being less severe if they compare it with the bizarre behavior exhibited by an autistic sibling or the publicly conspicuous appearance of a severely mentally retarded child who drools, walks with an abnormal gait, or is in a wheelchair. Such parents may see the acting-out child's problems as typical problems in a child of that age—problems that don't need any special attention. Some parents are too accepting and tolerant of acting-out behavior, either because they have guilty feelings that the acting out is caused by the family situation they have created, or because they lack the energy to deal with these difficulties. Some parents rationalize that at least the acting-out child (unlike the withdrawn child) is involved with the family, although in a negative way. Parents may to some extent mistake acting-out behavior as an exhibition of independence and free will. When parents ignore the basically disorganized and unhappy nature of such behavior, they run the risk of increasing the severity of the acting out.

Acting-Out Behavior

Copying the Handicapped Sibling's Problem Behavior

The earliest acting-out behavior may be apparent by the time a child is about eighteen months old. At this age, the ego of the toddler is still rather incompletely defined, and acting out may take the form of taking on those behaviors of the disabled sibling that earn him or her the most attention. If a hard-of-hearing mentally retarded older sister makes low, repetitive growling sounds, the mother may suddenly become aware that a younger sister is doing it, too—even though the mother has asked the older sister to stop the noises many times. A younger brother may echo his older brother's hyperactive behavior of running up and down the hall, screaming, and tumbling down the stairs. Initially, parents tend to react with a feeling of being overwhelmed by such copycat behavior, tempered with residual guilt that maybe it will turn out that the younger child has a similar problem—or, more likely, that the younger child thinks this is the only way to get attention.

The most strident example I've seen started with two-and-a-half-year-old Barry, an autistic boy, being held down screaming for twenty minutes while behavioral trainers worked to shape his behavior into complying with a request to put a block in a box.

After all the commotion subsided and Barry was given a break (during which he fled from his chair), his one-and-a-half-year-old sister, Clara, walked up to the same chair and, looking around at the several adults in the room, lifted her skirts and plopped herself on the same chair with a wicked smile. She too wanted a turn at this attention-getting maneuver!

When a child's acting-out behavior takes the form of conducting himself or herself similarly to the developmentally disabled sibling, the child is, in effect, saying to himself or herself, "This bad behavior seems to work for my brother. Perhaps it will work to get attention for me as well." If, without offering an explanation, the parents then discipline the child for the same acting-out behaviors that the disabled sibling gets away with, they will set the stage for more resentment and anger. It is important that, in situations like these, the parents are able to treat the unaffected child as an ally, honestly attribute the disabled sibling's behavior to his or her disorder (as well as the child can understand), and explain that that is the only reason they tolerate it. Sometimes, parents are hesitant to "label" a disabled sibling's behavior as being part of his or her disorder. Somehow, the process of labeling the behavior draws the line between personality and illness. The truth is that children readily perceive where this line should be drawn, and parental denial of the distinction further keeps the acting-out child from being in touch with his or her own perceptions and feelings.

Causing Temper Tantrums in the Handicapped Sibling

Early in their lives, acting-out children are likely to engage in behavior and activities that provoke temper tantrums in their disabled sibling. On another occasion, Clara, the little girl in the previous example, suffered several rejections in her attempts to get her brother Barry's attention while he carefully ordered and lined up alphabet blocks. Clara ran up and grabbed a couple of letters from the middle of Barry's line, bringing them triumphantly to me, while Barry screamed and flapped his hands at his disrupted row of blocks. With siblings of autistic children, acting out often takes the form of disturbing carefully lined up objects or otherwise thwarting routines or rituals that the autistic child insists on. Other mentally retarded children, who may be very attached to a particular toy, may experience grief from an acting-out sibling who deliberately provokes them by taking away the special object or damaging it.

At slightly older ages, acting-out siblings become wiser about directly acting out against the handicapped sibling in a way that will result in their parents' reprimanding or punishing them. For example, normal siblings may provoke the developmentally disabled child into doing something wrong, knowing the sibling will get into trouble. They learn to exploit the poor judgment, impulsivity, and eagerness to go along with peers that the retarded child shows. They may choose to do something that the disabled sibling frequently does wrong anyway, like forgetting to flush the toilet, leaving the TV on in another part of the house, or tearing bits of paper into little pieces and spreading them around. When confronted by the parent about who did what wrong, acting-out siblings may accuse the disabled sibling of these shortcomings, adding insult to injury by saying, "He did too! And he doesn't even remember!"

How do acting-out children develop their pattern of behavior? Some of it probably comes from personality or temperament, but another contributing factor may be being assigned the role of family scapegoat for minor transgressions. These children may be accused of bringing on the tantrums of the disabled sibling and may therefore be blamed for worsening his or her condition. A young enough child (under six) may really believe that teasing or tormenting a disabled sibling *is* the cause of his or her difference from other children. For young children this belief can both bring an exaggerated sense of their own power and conflicting feelings of guilt and remorse.

Externalizing versus Internalizing Anger

Acting out is a more primitive form of coping than becoming parentified, yet to a certain extent, it may be healthier than internalizing anger and turning it against oneself with unrealistic demands for perfectionism, or with self-punishment for minor or imagined transgressions against others or standards set for oneself. (In Chapter 9, we discuss some of these issues in more depth in the context of children who compensate by becoming superachievers.)

When children are acting out, they are openly expressing their anger toward their handicapped sibling. This expression may take the form of verbal resentment of the restrictions being imposed on their family life. It may also take the form of being physically aggressive toward the developmentally disabled sibling, or toward another family member who tries to control the children's behavior in their interactions with their sibling. Expressing oneself and one's needs is healthy from the point of view that the pent-up emotions do not result in accumulated internalized stress. With children who act out, a key step in facilitating a transition from maladaptive to adaptive behavior is to validate what they are feeling and to assist them in discovering more appropriate modes of expression. This approach may include getting them to say why they feel angry at their sibling, or why they feel jealous. It also requires that the parents be prepared to make some move in the direction of accommodating to the nonhandicapped children's feelings as a reward for their efforts to express themselves more positively. For example, if a seven-year-old hides his ten-year-old retarded brother's favorite stuffed animal and won't say where it is, his mother might cajole him to tell by asking what he's trying to get back at his brother for. If the seven-year-old will tell (or the mother can guess) the reason—for example, they had to leave the park early because the ten-year-old was having a tantrum when no one would play with him—the mother might offer a solo trip to the park for the seven-year-old if he will get the stuffed animal and apologize to his brother.

If this type of intervention takes place early, these children are likely to grow up with the necessary skills for striking an appropriate balance between caring for themselves and giving of themselves. One of the most important steps in such an intervention is to identify the situation in which the acting-out child is most likely to misbehave, and to deal with the roots of the problem, not just the behavior, that is, to find a way of giving the acting-out child some extra attention while she or he is still being good. Accentuating the positive, while deemphasizing the negative, nurtures the acting-out child when she or he needs it most and also takes away the reinforcement value she or he may get from acting bad.

Acting Out through School Failure

In the worst cases, where the child gets attention only for acting bad, acting-out behavior may begin to extend beyond family life and may become a more pervasive problem. These children are certainly at risk of continuing this behavior at school and eventually being seen as chronic underachievers. Sometimes, being an underachiever is a way of taking a sense of successful parenting away from parents who crave it badly in order to compensate for the deficiencies of their developmentally disabled child. Sometimes, however, school failure is a direct effect of being ignored and lacking parental help in developing skills needed for success in school. Glen Kovak was a seventh-grader when things came to a head with his sixteen-year-old, six-foot, 225-pound severely retarded brother, David. David would grab Glen's homework off the kitchen table, frequently tearing it to shreds. In the absence of effective parental intervention (Mrs. Kovak would just tell Glen, "It isn't David's fault. He doesn't know any better."), Glen moved into the garage. He was acting out being a nonperson, a message that was unfortunately lost on his parents. Although Glen's behavior could also classify him as a withdrawn child, his actions bespoke a loud and clear message to his parents.

Acting-out behavior that is reflected in school failure may eventually be brought to the parents' attention by school officials, who may or may not have any way of understanding its causes. The result is that the child finally gets his or her parents' attention, but for the wrong reasons. Unfortunately, this attention often sets the acting-out child up to repeat this failure in order to get additional attention from his or her parents.

As in other domains of behavior, if the acting-out child is doing poorly in school as a means of gaining attention, it is even more important for the parents to give praise and positive feedback for activities and accomplishments that they would otherwise take for granted. Once a cycle of negative behavior used to gain any attention is set up, it is difficult to break.

Clinically, it often appears that a family with an acting-out child is a family with an acting-out parent. Acting-out parents may be unnecessarily abusive to teachers and social workers who are trying to help them with their handicapped child, and they may fail to obtain services for their child because they are offered only services that are palliative and not curative.

Characteristics of the Acting-Out Child

Expressing Anger

Acting-out children often show overt anger and hostility toward their disabled sibling. As mentioned, this acting-out often takes the form of deliberately engaging in behavior that will "set off" the disabled child. Acting-out children may also refuse to cooperate in the usual household chores, to go to bed on time, or to do any of the other things required of them. When asked to follow rules from which the developmentally disabled sibling is exempt, they will protest loudly. It is important for parents to carefully evaluate the fairness of the exceptions they make for their disabled child. For example, a mentally retarded child may take twice as long to help clear the table as another child. However, if the other children feel that their disabled sibling's exemption from clearing the table is a privilege, there are likely to be hard feelings. In this situation, it is important for someone to help the retarded child do his or her share so that the siblings won't feel taken advantage of. (In fact, it is good for the adaptive behavioral development of the retarded child that he or she be made to help.) The key is to validate the acting-out child's feelings while explaining the situation and setting up appropriate ground rules.

Testing limits is the rule for children who respond to frustration by acting out toward their disabled sibling or their parents. Although the parents are indeed advised to set limits, they should be tempered with genuine validation of the pain, anger, and frustration that the children are feeling. Such children may set up situations to test whether their parents will apply different standards to them and to their handicapped sibling. One possible explanation for such behavior is that these children are trying to reassure themselves that they are *not* the same as their handicapped sibling and so are seeking special dispensations for *their* unacceptable behavior, just as the disabled sibling is given special dispensations for his or her limitations. Thus, acting-out children create their own identity in the family based on *their* negative traits, much as they perceive the disabled sibling to be doing the same.

Who Is at Risk of Becoming an Acting-Out Child?

The Acting-Out Child and Family Characteristics

Younger children tend to have more primitive defenses and may be the most likely to cope by acting out. In addition, a system is probably already in place for the care of the disabled child before the birth of much younger children, making it less necessary for them to play an active role in caring for the disabled sibling and thus decreasing their chance of becoming parentified. As is the case in any family, by the time the younger children arrive, the parents have already been "broken in" by the older children. The younger children can therefore get away with much more, and their acts of provocation will be tolerated and ignored more readily.

In general, boys are more likely than girls to act out. Social expectations push girls more readily into the caretaking role of the parentified child, and even into the role of superachievers. The general "boys will be boys" or machismo attitude prevalent in many cultures pushes males into coping, although maladaptively, by acting out.

Maladaptive Behavior

Acting-out children, because they are active, and because they can externalize stress, may be more likely later on to assert their own needs and to take care of themselves. The key is to help them learn to temper their overreactive behavior with compassion and consideration for others. This is best accomplished by *not* punishing them for asserting their own needs, and at the same time showing them that they *will* be punished for hurting others, especially their disabled sibling.

Numbed Emotions

Some acting-out children are able to commit antisocial acts because they simply do not feel remorse or much of anything. Such children have been described as having numbed emotions. These are often the result of being told that one's feelings are wrong or that one's feelings are the opposite of what they are. For example, imagine the following scene: A five-year-old brother is building a block castle. His seven-year-old mentally retarded brother, uninvited, "helps" and knocks it all over. The five-year-old takes a swing at the seven-year-old, the seven-year-old cries, and the five-year-old says, "I hate you!" The mother, realizing that the problem occurred because of the seven-year-old's poor coordination (and not because of ill intentions) says angrily to the five-year-old, "You don't hate your brother; you love him! Hug him and make up." At that moment, all the five-year-old feels is hate. The mother should not deny the five-year-old's angry feelings but should separate the feeling about what happened from the responsible party. She could say, "Your brother is clumsy; he can't help it when he does that. Why don't you build over here on the table, and I'll keep him away." Young children, like the five-year-old in the example, do not yet have a fully evolved internal monitor that can tell them for sure what is right from wrong. A child who acts out needs to have his angry feelings acknowledged and validated, not denied out of existence. A child who is told that he is feeling "love" at the very moment when he is feeling "hate" will not develop a reliable internal monitor. After a while, his gauge for right and wrong will probably be the answer to the question, "Can I get away with it?" Numbed emotions can result when others outside of the self fail to validate what is going on inside.

Problems in Adolescence

Acting-out problems may get worse with age. What starts out as a mild behavior problem at school may result in juvenile delinquency in adolescence. Acting-out children have a strong need to be the center of attention, both within and outside the home. If acting out at home brings the desired attention, acting out in school and socially, via drug or alcohol use and other antisocial behavior, may follow as the child enters adolescence. When an adolescent with a tendency to act out stress meets with rejection at home, his or her self-esteem is often deflated, and that adolescent may seek prestige outside the family instead. Unlike the super-achieving sibling, who manages to garner positive attention outside the home, the acting-out child garners negative attention, which results in worsening self-esteem and an even greater increase in the desire for more extrafamilial recognition. But it must be emphasized that all this acting-out behavior, both in and outside the home, is most likely a result of an attempt to draw attention away from the disabled sibling. The negative attention received is attention nevertheless, and it fulfills an emotional need, although in a distorted way.

Helping the Acting-Out Child

Acknowledging the Acting-Out Child's Emotions

It is one thing to say that an acting-out child needs to receive positive attention before he or she starts to act badly. It is another thing to give that attention. Such an intervention is extremely difficult for parents who are already dealing with the hardships of having an autistic child. Coping with the further strain of a child who is acting out may be too much; the parents may not have much patience with this added frustration and may just lash out in anger, without validating the child's feelings. What acting-out children need most is to have their underlying emotions brought to the surface and validated by being discussed as real concerns. Denying that the bad behavior is a reaction to family stress further negates for acting-out children the possibility that their problems will ever be fairly addressed by their parents.

Parentally Sanctioned Forms of Acting Out

Occasionally, parents realize that they are strongly identifying with the hostile wishes that one of their normal children seems to be acting out on the disabled child. The parents themselves may be dealing with negative fantasies about their disabled child, like imagining how they might react if a fatal accident befell the child, or what their lives would be like if the child had simply never been born. Some parents, through awareness of their own frustrations, can appreciate how the nondisabled siblings can be helped to feel less helpless when they are victimized by the disabled sibling. Lydia Waller, the mother of four-year-old Anna and two-year-old Ezra, who is autistic, described this situation perfectly. Late one afternoon, she said, when the three of them were all cranky, Ezra pulled Anna's curly blond ringlets for about the fifth time. Instead of giving Anna her fifth "turn-the-other-cheek" lecture of the day, Lydia said, "OK, go ahead, you can pull Ezra's hair" (fair retribution in the eyes of any four-year-old). Anna yanked, Ezra cried— and he never tried to pull Anna's hair again. In this case, Lydia was wise enough to realize that Anna's idea of fairness (which was to pull Ezra's hair) and Lydia's adult idea of fairness (to turn the other cheek) were at odds, and that if Anna was not to feel abused, Anna would need an opportunity to reestablish an equilibrium with her brother on terms she understood.

Family Therapy

Dealing with persistent acting-out behavior in a child is difficult enough for any parent; for those who also have a disabled child, it is quite reasonable to look for professional assistance. At first glance, some may see acting out as solely the child's problem and refer him or her to individual therapy for a "cure." Sending a child to an individual therapist while the rest of the family goes untreated, however, is likely to exacerbate the problem by increasing this child's feelings of isolation when just the opposite is needed. In the worst case, parents, friends, and perhaps other family members may see this child's behavior as the cause of the family's problems and maybe even as something that worsens the disabled child's condition, for example, "If he (the acting-out child) would only leave his brother alone and not antagonize him, he would be alright." Parental statements and attitudes like this one tend to increase the acting-out child's sense of isolation and also foster feelings of guilt. Parents who are themselves acting out may say such things to their nonhandicapped children to displace their own anger at their disabled child onto another child, who they unconsciously feel should be more able to take it.

When there is an acting-out child in the family, the behavioral problems are often more global, involving all members of the family, who are enmeshed in a complex network of causes and effects. Professional intervention should include family therapy (preferably with a therapist familiar with the problems brought about by having a disabled child in the family). To a degree, acting-out children are reacting normally to an abnormal situation. But they must also learn that their behavior may have a negative effect on others whom they do not want to hurt. Anger may just be acting-out children's best way of communicating thoughts and bad feelings that they are not fully aware of themselves. Therapy may help families to see this and to take steps to alleviate the stresses that are causing their children's reaction. Being in therapy together may also enhance a family's awareness that the disabled child's presence makes life more difficult for all—directly or indirectly. This awareness may increase family cohesiveness, decrease divisiveness, and create new alliances. Individual therapy for the acting-out child may be a good idea, but family therapy may be more important.

Conclusions

In the next chapter, we discuss a final prototype for children's coping with a developmentally disabled sibling: superachievement. Like the acting-out child, the superachieving child may turn away from the home to look for attention, validation, and gratification. However, the superachieving child strives to get others to notice how good he or she is, not how bad.

Chapter 9

The Superachieving Child

Superachieving and Perfectionism

Some siblings of disabled children develop a style of coping that is focused on being perfect. In this way, they can prove to their parents that they are just the opposite of the sibling who causes all the family distress. The superachieving child needs to demonstrate that he or she not only is not developmentally disabled but in fact can compensate the parents for the disabled child's shortcomings by being well above average. Superachieving children are similar to parentified and acting-out children in that they, too, externalize their feelings of conflict and anxiety by extreme behavior. Whereas parentified children excel in activities related to their developmentally disabled sibling, superachieving children excel in activities outside the family. Some siblings attempt to be both parentified and superachieving. These children seek to be perfect both inside and outside the home, often subjecting themselves to unrealistically high standards. Some children start out exhibiting parentified patterns of behavior when younger and, as they mature, transfer the drive for approval from just their parents to others outside the home, such as a teacher or a coach; thus, they become superachievers in school, music, sports, or some other arena. In this chapter, we focus on the preconditions and influences for becoming a superachieving child, and we give some examples of families in which children have become superachievers for different reasons. We also focus on how superachieving siblings can be differentiated from parentified siblings, as well as on how their issues overlap.

One may ask, "What's wrong with striving for an extremely high level of achievement?" The answer is, "Nothing." The motivation and the emotional stress involved are the issue. Hard work and accomplishments can be wonderful. However, children from families with a disabled child often work excessively hard in order to fill a void that has been created by the accomplishments their sibling will never attain.

Superachieving children feel that they have to do extra well; this is the only way they can get attention from their parents and other significant people in their life. And they do as well as they do, not only to grab the attention of their parents, but also to make the parents themselves feel good, to make them feel whole, and to make them not feel like failures for having a handicapped child. These goals can amount to quite a burden for a child. Established in childhood, this pattern is set up for life; the child becomes a severely driven adult to whom any form of failure is devastating.

Giving birth to a child with a disability may make parents question how able they are to be parents and whether they made a mistake in having children. The most natural response is to look to the disabled child's siblings for validation that they can create children who are not only normal but gifted. In our clinic, many parents ask whether it is true that the siblings of autistic children are more often intellectually gifted. Although this subject has never been carefully studied, the answer seems to lie more in the fact that the parents notice such a vast discrepancy in intellectual functioning between their disabled child and their normal children, and that signs of intelligence in the normal siblings are carefully noted because they allay the parents' fear that they can't create normal children. To some extent, parents choose to have children to perpetuate an essential part of themselves. Parents naturally wish their offspring to be incarnate versions of themselves—only better. When it becomes clear that the parents' fantasies about their children being reflections of themselves will not be fulfilled by the disabled child, they make an even larger emotional investment in the success of the siblings.

The Mental Age Gap

As time passes, the "mental" age gap between a developmentally disabled child and his or her normal siblings widens. This occurs whether the developmentally disabled sibling is younger or older than the normal child. For example, if the disabled child is moderately retarded and two years old, her or his mental age may be that of a one-year-old. If a normal sibling is four, there is a three-year mental age difference. However, by the time the children are six and eight years old, the moderately retarded child, still maturing at half the expected rate, will have a mental age of three years, whereas her or his sibling will have a mental age of eight years, and there will be a five-year gap. In some families, the widening gap tends to be seen as unusually accelerated growth in the normal child, rather than as slow growth in the disabled child. If the parents perceive their children's relative growth this way, they are able to see the disabled child as relatively less slow and less handicapped and the normal child as relatively more advanced than most others of the same age. This overidealization of the capacity of the normal child puts pressure on that child to fulfill the parental ideal. The child may also internalize that standard, believing that he or she does have extraspecial capacities, and that the onus is on him or her to use these abilities as well as possible. The child may or may not actually be above average, but the burden to meet above-average standards becomes set. In this way, the superachieving child's accomplishments become an overcompensation for the shortcomings of the disabled sibling.

Superachieving children learn to seek outside markers of success to make up for the lack of reinforcement from within the family. They are at risk of having a very weak internal sense of success, which may lead to perfectionistic tendencies—the feeling that they would feel better if they were better at what they were doing, and that good is not good enough. Superachievers often suffer from the "missing tile syndrome"; that is, they may see an elaborate, beautifully tiled floor or ceiling, and instead of being impressed by the intricate design or detail, their eyes are immediately drawn to the space where one tile (out of thousands) is missing. They can't enjoy the overall beauty because of the one small flaw. As adults, such individuals may have a difficult time enjoying successes; nothing ever really feels as if it's enough. After one accomplishment, he or she is off to the next. The constant need to be busy and to go from one thing to the next also allows superachievers to ward off negative feelings about their family (and their true feelings of self-worth), which may have been walled off in early childhood.

The Importance of Being Independent

Another way in which superachievers gain praise is by not needing any help. This lack of need may reassure parents that the superachieving child is naturally talented. It also counterbalances some of the pressure and extra work the parents must do to take care of their disabled child. In psychodynamic terms, this is a "reaction formation," in which the child functions in opposition to the sibling's defectiveness. Superachieving children learn never to ask for help. In fact, a hallmark of superachievers is that their parents may see them as already knowing everything they need to know. On several occasions when I have suggested sibling support groups for anxious, superachieving children, their parents have responded positively, saying, "What a great idea! Sara (or Melissa or Joshua) has so much she can *teach* the other siblings!" Such parents entirely miss the point that I am suggesting that the sibling *get* help rather than *give* it. Because the parents themselves are often in no position to help with schoolwork or personal problems, these children grow up feeling that they must always rely only on themselves. One hallmark of the superachieving child is premature independence. For example, in our clinic, a superachieving third-grader volunteered to wait alone in a waiting room for three hours, reading a book, while her sibling and her parent were to go off to some unknown location in our big hospital building. In this case, the sibling's offer was backed up by the parent, who said, "Jill is a super reader. She has two books with her, and she'll be just fine!" (We took Jill along with us anyway.)

Expressions of premature independence may manifest themselves at a very early age and may be at least partly a result of walling oneself off from a sibling who is very negatively intrusive and who makes being alone a relatively attractive alternative. The "aloneness" that the child learns to accept may be both internal and emotional as well as external, as just described. For example, Katy, age four, was easily one of the most picture-perfect blonde-ringleted little girls I have ever seen. Her brother, Nicholas, was a wild moderately retarded ten-year-old boy who was in the hospital in the hope of finding an antipsychotic medication that would quell his unpredictable violent outbursts. While I was standing and talking to Katy's mom in a hallway, Nicholas suddenly removed his sneaker and flung it, for no obvious reason, from close range at Katy's face. Tears silently flowed down Katy's face, as she looked up at her mom and in a quiet voice reported, "Nicky hit me." Somewhere along the line, Katy had learned not to react as emotionally as one might expect to such severe aggression by a sibling. She did not demand that her mom exact retribution from Nicky, nor did she even cry to be picked up. Such an early overcontrolled emotional response may be one predictor of coping with distress, by not reacting with anger or frustration, but by showing a perfect, almost saintly response.

Not only must superachievers be self-reliant, but as they grow up, they come to realize that others are relying on their successes as well. And because without successes superachievers feel they are not worthy of being loved, they have difficulties developing feelings of intrinsic self-worth outside the achievements that parents can enumerate as proof of their exceptionality.

Like parentified children, superachievers are by no means the squeaky wheel, and therefore, they don't get any of the oil—in fact, they are the oil for their own wheels. Unfortunately, even fully functioning wheels still need periodic maintenance so they don't wear out. We live in a society in which achievement and accomplishment are highly valued. People who sacrifice themselves for their work are often seen in a positive light, even as role models to be emulated. Without emotional support and positive feedback for accomplishments, however, superachieving children can falter, too, and may eventually begin to "squeak" themselves. Even when superachievers are not nurtured emotionally, they are still expected to accomplish new things. Their talents are seen as being as "inborn" as their sibling's defects.

Whereas the parents may feel good about having a child whose successes prove that they can indeed raise a normal, very-high-functioning child, they often take his or her accomplishments as a given and fail to give adequate positive feedback. There may be a number of reasons. First, failure to give praise may help reinforce the parents' feelings that the nondisabled child is naturally bright, that is, that his or her aptitudes come directly from his or her genetic endowment. Second, praising the superachieving child further "unevens" the score of the praises and punishments that are meted out to the nondisabled and disabled children—making the disabled child look even more defective. Third, the parents may feel that praise will spoil the child and deter him or her from trying hard in the future. This seems especially true of parents who must use strict behavioral approaches with their disabled child to keep negative behaviors in line. Fourth, the parents tend to imbue their nonhandicapped children with adultlike traits even before they are very mature at all, and feel that these children *know* they've done well, and that is reward enough (as it might be for an adult). For all of these reasons, superachievers may never receive the love and warmth that they so desperately seek. The result may be a cycle of filling the void by accomplishing more and more. This pattern is also a setup for a lot of disappointment in later life, as the superachiever seeks achievement after achievement in an effort to receive enough external markers of success to feel good. However, such individuals may have persisting problems in really "feeling" their own success, because early in their lives, it was never mirrored back to them by their parents.

The Need for a Separate Life Outside the Home

Unlike the parentified child, and more like the withdrawn child, the superachieving child may, over time, become increasingly detached from family activities. This detachment is not really an abdication of family responsibility, but the taking on of more significant roles outside the family. These may be leadership roles in school, a heavy sports schedule, or other extracurricular activities that involve being away from home for many nonschool hours. In this way, superachievers derive their measures of high status from outside the family in socially respected ways.

Unlike the parentified child, who is not overtly ashamed of his or her handicapped sibling, the superachieving child has a strong need to maintain two separate lives, one inside and one outside the home. Because perfection is highly valued by superachievers, they may be very reluctant to invite friends to the house, because the presence of a handicapped sibling would interfere with the perfect image they need to maintain. They may try to compartmentalize their emotions about their family and cut these emotions off from what they see as the "real" self that exists outside the home.

A very good example is the Golden family, who live in a rural back-to-the-1960s lifestyle. Mrs. Golden, a single parent, has four children: Tina and Tanya, who are eight and ten years old, and Alan and Alex, who are four and three years old. Alan is autistic and spends most of his time doing his own thing, like hanging naked from ropes in trees in the family garden. Mrs. Golden pursues a lifestyle of macrobiotic organic-vegetable consumption and homeopathic interventions for Alan while allowing him to create a home environment that is difficult for the other children to adapt to. Alan ties the furniture at home together with long ropes that he trails around the house, tantrumming if they are moved, and generally controls the family's mealtimes like a medium to large predatory animal. Without the help of any child welfare service, Tina and Tanya have basically moved themselves out of their home because of their circumstances. They have "adopted" themselves out to the homes of their best friends, where they often sleep and go after school. Both girls do well in school and are mature, sensible, and organized. When social workers interview them about the strange circumstances in their own home, they say, "Well, that's just Mom's thing. That's what Mom's like. She's OK, though."

The Hero or Mascot of the Family

In many ways, the superachieving child may function as the hero or the mascot of the family. He or she is the one everyone can point to and say, "See, we really aren't that bad. We've got him (or her) in the family; we must be doing something right." The family mascot may be the youngest child, and although less accomplished in school, sports, the arts, or some other domain, he or she is chosen to be the family's focus of attention when they are with others because he or she is a charmer, cute or funny, or with a very outgoing personality. Although parents may have difficulty praising their "mascot" child directly, they may be less hesitant in enumerating his or her accomplishments to relatives and friends outside the family. In this way, the parents can use the superachieving child to redeem their own sense of worth among those whom they imagine blame them for having produced a disabled child, too.

Intermittent Reinforcement of Achievements

In behavioral psychology, it is well known that one of the best ways to reinforce a behavior is with intermittent rather than continuous rewards. Basically, this is what often occurs with the superachieving child. Because of the demands of the developmentally disabled child, the parents cannot always be available for the nondisabled sibling. The availability of the parents is a function of the demands that the disabled sibling places on them, which is a factor out of the nondisabled child's control. Thus, a pattern of intermittent and unpredictable attention from their parents makes superachievers strive even harder for accomplishments that will get them noticed. Although intermittent reinforcement may increase achievement-oriented activity, it is not the most emotionally healthy means of self-motivation because it is not dependable.

Superachieving and Family Characteristics

Firstborn children are the most likely to become superachievers. Another prime candidate is the first child of the same sex who is born after the disabled child. Younger children may be more likely to take on the cute "mascot" role. Clinically, it seems that superachieving is more likely to occur among males, especially firstborn males, whereas firstborn females, as we discussed in Chapter 6, are more likely to become parentified.

The larger the family, the less often parents seem to point to any one child as *the* compensation for the disabled one. In a large family, just having a number of other kids who all seem "normal" seems to be adequate. Therefore, clinically, we more often see superachieving children in families with only two or three children.

Family spacing also seems to affect parental pressure to superachieve. A number of couples wait seven, eight, or more years after having a disabled child to try parenthood again. Often, the wait has been due to the fear of having another disabled child, and sometimes the wait is due to the sheer exhaustion associated with the early years of the disabled child's life. When the next child comes along this much later, the parents almost always have very high expectations for that child. In the best situations, that child gets more attention because the parents have begun to de-cathect from the disabled child to some extent. The Tylers have ten-year-old Carlos and two-year-old Sam. Carlos is a truly multi-handicapped child whose accumulated labels include mentally retarded, cerebral palsied, epileptic, hyperactive, apraxic, visually impaired, and autistic; he was more than the usual handful. The Tylers took a number of years to work up the courage to have another child. Within two years of Sam's birth, the developmental differences between the boys were already so apparent that the Tylers decided on residential placement for Carlos so that they could foster Sam's development and enjoy being with him after so many difficult years with Carlos. The Tylers explicitly stated their fear that if they did not seek residential placement for Carlos, Sam would get much less attention and might grow up feeling that he existed only to "prove" that his parents didn't produce just defec-tive children.

Implications for the Adult Sibling

Superachieving children probably become superachievers through a combination of predisposing personality factors, like a tendency to be perfectionistic and a little obsessive, combined with some of the family pressures we have described. Research has still shown relatively little about how character and personality factors interact with circumstances within the family to produce super-achieving children. Clearly, the child who responds to a disability in the family by becoming a superachiever may be making a more functional adaptation than a child who becomes withdrawn or depressed, or than one who acts out.

However, as adults, superachievers may find themselves struggling with a need to let go of the fine details in order to reduce life stress and to have more time just to "smell the roses." Especially at risk may be individuals from whom their parents have expected more than they could realistically deliver. Other at-risk individuals are those with parents who have defined their areas for achievement for them—perhaps excelling physically because their brother has cerebral palsy, or becoming a doctor because the parents have seen so many doctors who dashed their hopes of curing their disabled child's condition.

Sometimes through individual psychotherapy, and sometimes through a career change, adult siblings begin to resolve the need to superachieve enough to feel more comfortable with themselves, and to be less demanding of those around them. A realistic reappraisal of goals, in terms of both service to one's family and commitments outside the family may help.

Chapter 10

Promoting a Healthy Family Life

Adjustment to a Disabled Sibling as a Child and as an Adult

In this chapter, we focus on specific remedies for helping families cope with the day-to-day realities of living with a handicapped child and balancing the needs of disabled and nondisabled siblings. Our thesis is that nonhandicapped siblings who have a better childhood with their disabled brother or sister will have a better adulthood with them. Giving a non-handicapped child a happy childhood despite the added stressors on the family not only is important in its own right but is a central concern of many parents who want their nondisabled children, as adults, to feel good about taking responsibility for their handicapped brother or sister after the parents no longer can. Our philosophy is one of treating the developmentally disabled child as normally as possible and expecting whatever is developmentally appropriate behavior for his or her mental age and physical capacities. The nondisabled children have to make some allowances, but also need their parents to accede to them sometimes, too.

Not all families are "nuclear" in structure, especially in the 1990s. Nontraditional families now include those with single parents, families of divorce, blended and stepfamilies, and families of gay and lesbian parents. Any of these families may discover themselves having a disabled child and must deal with the associated problems. We mention this here because, although much of what we cover in this chapter and in this book seems to apply to the "traditional" nuclear family, the concepts we discuss are intended to apply to most families, irrespective of their composition.

The potential difficulties for families with a developmentally disabled child are numerous; as mentioned in earlier chapters, the nonhandicapped children of families with a disabled child are at risk of family isolation, parental neglect, guilt, shame, stigma, and questions about their own health and genetic makeup.

Changes in Normal Sibling Relationships

In relationships with siblings, children experience certain emotions for the first time that may influence their subsequent development and future relationships. Because siblings share the same parents and living space, it is through siblings that children naturally learn their first lessons about sharing and making sacrifices and about how to handle love, anger, ambivalence, conflict, hatred, loyalty, resentment, and empathy. As adults, siblings have the potential to serve as wonderful companions and "reality checks" in times of crisis, because they share one's personal history as nobody else does. In the best circumstances, this arrangement works out well, and siblings live happily as close friends for life. But this is often not the case, even in the absence of a disabled sibling as a complicating factor. Siblings may have very different personalities; they often don't relate to each other well and sometimes don't even speak with each other much. Childhood competitions and resentments may have been left unresolved. When your sibling is disabled, all bets are likely to be off: The relationship and relationship history are more often a one-way street, and the benefits of mutual maturation do not exist. Nevertheless, you remain siblings, and contact with your disabled sibling as an adult may provoke images of childhood, just as it does with nondisabled siblings.

Although sibling relationships between developmentally disabled adults and their brothers and sisters can often be characterized as a one-way street, the relationship may be an altruistic one, and one in which the normal siblings are gratified by being able to do helpful things that honor the wishes of elderly or deceased parents. An example of coming to accept the one-way-street relationship was poignantly demonstrated in our clinic one day by the visit of fifty-six-year-old Tommy, a moderately retarded mute man, who was brought by his younger twin brothers, also in their fifties. Tommy lived in a group home in the town where he'd grown up, which was about thirty-five miles away from one brother and four hundred miles away from the other, who had flown in to help his twin with Tommy's doctor's appointment. Both brothers were quite successful financially, and when they went to visit Tommy, they always brought him new clothes that were of the same quality as the well-tailored leisure wear they both wore. Tommy's great pleasure in seeing either of his brothers was the knowledge that he'd be taken out for a hamburger. At the beginning of the interview, one of the twins went out to the hospital cafeteria, returning with two burgers, two bags of fries, and two Haagen-Dazs ice cream bars. I thought they were going to have lunch. Instead, one brother gently tucked several napkins into the collar of Tommy's new tennis shirt and pushed up the sleeves of his new wool cardigan, while the other cut the burgers in half and laid out catsup next to the fries. It took Tommy the next hour to eat it all, but he finished it. In the interview, it seemed apparent that the altruism the twins were able to show for their brother was probably due at least in part to the fact that Tommy's parents had always seen Tommy as retarded and different but had not neglected the younger boys while they were all growing up. Both the twins (and apparently the parents while they were still living) had had a realistic view of Tommy's differences and limitations all along, and the family's philosophy had been to allow Tommy to gently coexist alongside his brothers.

Situations like the one we've just described make it clear that the quality of the adult relationship between affected and non-affected siblings is strongly related to how the family has handled the inevitable difficulties that have arisen throughout development. Studies have shown that it is the family's acceptance of the disability, and not the nature or the severity of the disability itself, that has the greatest impact on how the other children in the family adjust. It is very important for parents to take an active role in opening the channels of communication with their children and between their children.

For example, early on, the normal siblings may come to resent playing with their developmentally disabled sibling because the "play" can consist of the disabled sibling's wrecking whatever the nondisabled siblings have set up. It is quite expectable for the normal siblings to declare that they "hate" their brother or sister, and that they don't want to play with him or her. It's important for parents to help the normal children in that situation to draw a distinction between hating to have their play wrecked and hating the sibling who is doing the wrecking, especially if the sibling cannot be made to understand what she or he is doing wrong. Parents who keep the channels of communication open allow the nondisabled children to express their feelings of frustration (rather than deny them) and also show empathy by not insisting that the disabled sibling always be included in the nondisabled siblings' activities.

Until adolescence, children need opportunities to talk about their feelings in context, as in the situation just described. It is very difficult to sit children under ten or twelve down to talk generally or abstractly about the emotional issues engendered by their disabled sibling. Children may also not be ready to talk about important emotional issues when the parents are ready, but it is important for children to know that it is OK to talk, whenever *they* are ready, and that they will be allowed to express their thoughts and feelings without being judged negatively for them. In showing openness and willingness to listen and talk about feelings as they come up, parents set the tone and open lines of honest communication that can endure. In this chapter, we outline some issues that families find helpful to consider and discuss with each other—and sometimes with professionals—in order to adjust better to having a disabled child in the family.

Stressors That Affect Family Functioning

How will the siblings of disabled children end up as adults? Will they grow up full of anger and resentment? Will this wrath be buried, or will it be evident on the surface? Will they prove genuinely more compassionate and caring, reflecting fondly on difficult experiences that truly brought their family closer together? Will they recognize their own ambivalence and realize that one can be compassionate and giving without being totally self-sacrificing? Will they recognize that anger, love, and resentment can all coexist in the same person, and that this coexistence is OK? Having a disabled sibling provides a wonderful chance to establish and nurture positive and rare qualities in oneself. Yet, many siblings become totally self-sacrificing or swallowed up in anger. Others grow up denying their feelings and simply state that their sibling was there.

Ensuring a healthy family coping style and approach, however, is easier said than done. As we pointed out in Chapter 3, nobody expects to have a child with a developmental disability, and therefore the potential problems are not anticipated and planned for. In our model, an emotionally healthy family with a developmentally disabled child is able to cope by living in much the same way that they might if the disabled sibling were normal.

Maintaining a normal family life is difficult, but not impossible. Acknowledgment of the difficulty is the first step. Acceptance of outside advice and help is often the second. A healthy family should serve certain functions for its members. A healthy, functional family is one in which problems are anticipated and/or are dealt with when they arise. The family should foster growth and a feeling of security among all its members.

Baseline Ability to Cope

Even before the birth of a child with a disability, families and individuals vary considerably in their baseline ability to cope with problems. Some families can communicate and handle stress well; others fall apart. And even the strongest families have a threshold beyond which their ability to cope declines.

Changes in Family Function with Time

According to experience, most families experience the most stress when the developmentally disabled child is first diagnosed. As mentioned earlier, in the first year after diagnosis, signs of depression are common in one or both parents. In addition, the presence of other infants and toddlers demands that the parents pay much attention to their family life. For many families, the situation calms down when the disabled child and the other children are all old enough to be in school full time. Another turning point is when the disabled child (and his or her siblings) reaches adolescence. In mentally retarded children, the physical urges of adolescence are accompanied by a lack of inhibition and a tendency to discharge nasty hormonal storms in physical abuse (rather than in verbal abuse, as in most other teenagers). Family dynamics may change as the nondisabled adolescents naturally become interested in spending more time outside the home. Still another turning point occurs when the nondisabled siblings leave home as young adults, and the parents often face the possibility of placing the disabled child in some sort of residential care facility (if they haven't already).

Support systems and strategies for coping that may have worked during one period in the life cycle do not always work at other times. For a two-year-old nondisabled sibling, being able to count on having a story read each night at bedtime may be a critical part of a routine that builds trust in the parents. A ten-year-old may need to be able to count on at least one parent's making it to each soccer game. Having evening respite care so the parents and the nondisabled teenagers can go out to the movies and pizza together on a Sunday night may be important. However, by college age, a young adult returning home may want to have a whole weekend alone with her or his parents, and the parents need to be flexible enough to be able to provide that time. The principle is that the parents should strive to find ways of maintaining a degree of contact with their nondisabled children that is similar to the contact that other children of the same age expect of their parents. It is realistic to expect that flexibility to be compromised, and the frequency of time together to be somewhat diminished, but it is important that the quality of the parents' time with the nondisabled children be high when there is time for them to be together.

Over the years, the family's need to maintain its capacity to resolve problems remains a constant. As long as a disabled child lives at home, adjustments usually have to be made. An awareness of just how the disabled child's presence affects the lifestyle of the rest of the family is important. Good problem-solving skills will help the family deal with crises and changes. These skills involve being able to enumerate alternate ways of conducting family life and coming up with solutions that offer compromises for everyone (including the disabled child).

The use of formal support systems outside the home, like respite care, day care centers, parent groups, and developmental disabilities professionals, can also promote adaptive solutions where there is apparently not enough time or ideas to address a family's problem situations. Parents who obtain more information on the disability affecting their child and on the available resources are in a better position to cope. Families that do not use the available supports tend to cope more poorly.

Suggestions for Coping with Areas of Family Conflict

Humor and Coping

The notion of using humor to cope with a disability usually raises eyebrows. After all, doesn't this constitute making fun of someone's disability, laughing at someone else's expense? The answer is yes and no. "Yes," if the humor is used to hurt, but if it is used to relieve the stress of living with a disabled child, then it is appropriate and may even provide the necessary space and perspective to solve problems effectively. For example, at a conference on autism, I recall hearing a parent describe being in a supermarket when her autistic child began to act out and disrupt the neatly stacked items on display. She told the child, "Now you stop that. You know that when I take you home, your mother is going to be extremely angry." This comment provided the necessary comic relief for her other children. Other parents use humorous descriptions of symptoms to deemphasize their abnormality, such as referring to hand flapping as attempts to fly, or to constant rocking as listening to an invisible Walkman. In each of these cases, the family members are aware that the behavior is atypical, but they tolerate it more easily by giving it a lighter meaning.

Limiting Child Care Responsibilities

Limiting child care responsibilities is particularly important in a small family, where the responsibilities cannot be spread out. Even in families with a parentified child who is most eager to volunteer for all sorts of caregiving activities, it is important to limit this child's obligations so that he or she has time to pursue developmentally appropriate activities. Parents need to bear in mind the mental age of the disabled child. Most parents would not ordinarily send a nine-year-old into the street to be responsible for a three-year-old child. Yet this is exactly what happens when parents ask a nine-year-old to look after a mentally retarded child who is twelve years old chronologically but three years old developmentally. Nondisabled children should not be made to feel guilty when they object to watching their brother or sister too often, or for excessive periods of time.

Being Alone with Parents

Expressing wishes to do things without the developmentally disabled sibling should be considered normal. Just as it is normal for older siblings to want time alone with their parents for their big-girl or big-boy activities when they have a nondisabled younger sibling, it is normal for them to have the same feelings about their disabled sibling. We are not implying that the developmentally disabled child should always be left behind or left out, just that some of the time, the nondisabled child needs to feel that it is right for his or her desires to take preference over those of a handicapped brother or sister, just as they would if his or her brother or sister were not disabled.

How do parents accomplish this time alone? Sometimes they accomplish it by forgoing family outings that include everyone, and instead, only one parent takes the nondisabled children for simple activities that their sibling may not be mature enough for, like sitting through a Disney movie or having dinner at Denny's. Because most young nondisabled siblings, like all younger children, prefer to have their parents together (assuming they have a two-parent family), using respite care or help from a relative, a neighbor, a church member, or a teacher's aide who can handle the disabled child's special needs may occasionally be the solution. It is also important to require the disabled child to do as much for herself or himself as possible, and to behave in a way that is up to her or his developmental capacity.

Each child needs some undivided, protected parental attention. This may mean telling the disabled child in front of his or her sibling, "I'm with Jeremy now. You're going to have to wait your turn." This action is good for the emotional health of the non-disabled sibling and may also help modify the social approach behavior of the disabled child, who may have difficulty reading more subtle social cues.

Parents need to set aside time to spend alone with each child. Such time alone gives each child the feeling that she or he matters, and that all the time is not monopolized by the disabled sibling. Parents should reinforce and validate the needs of the other children. Family gatherings and vacations should include some that focus on each child's interest or age level. Each child needs regular attention on a daily basis, even if it's just a short period of time that's just for him or her.

Occasionally, a family should go on outings without the handicapped child, so that the other siblings have some completely typical experiences that are just for them. If the family is going to attend a school or sporting event that includes one of the unaffected children, that child should help decide whether the disabled child would really be happy coming along. If it is a really special event for the unaffected sibling, like a graduation, a recital, or a starring role in a school play, the parents should leave the decision entirely to the sibling. All children need to feel that they are the total center of attention once in a while.

Issues of Space and Time

Although we realize that having a separate bedroom for each child often isn't possible, the size of the space isn't as important as the principle. Thus, parents may give the developmentally disabled child his or her own room so that there is less disruption in the other children's lives and possessions. Or the parents may set aside a portion of the home for certain hours of the day during which that space belongs to a certain child; he or she can do homework here, play, watch TV uninterrupted, or entertain friends. This sense of the ownership of a certain space also encourages a responsible attitude toward that space, that is, keeping it clean, and so on. Even if a child shares a room with a disabled sibling, he or she should have the room to himself or herself sometimes, in order to maintain privacy. A child who has to share a room with a disabled sibling and who never has any space to call his or her own may well abdicate all responsibility for taking care of that room because he or she figures, "Why should I bother cleaning up my room when it only gets messed up by my sibling?" Siblings who share rooms often are closer than other brothers and sisters. The child who has to share a room with the disabled sibling may feel that he or she is being put (unfairly) in a position of greater responsibility.

Treating Siblings Equally

Disabled children make demands and play off parents' guilt and vulnerability just as all children do to get their own way. But parents' favoring the disabled child is obviously going to look unfair to the healthy children, and no child can be expected to have the maturity to just brush off the hurt feelings that ensue. Sometimes favoritism is inevitable.

Fights between siblings are a normal part of everyday life in all families, including those with a disabled child. However, there may be a strong tendency for the parents to side with the disabled sibling and expect the other children to compromise. Some parents may expect the healthy child to be responsible *always* for cleaning up after play, while the disabled child never is. This favoritism can lead to resentment, not only toward the parents, but also toward the disabled sibling. Parents need to be sure to require the developmentally disabled child to behave up to standards that are developmentally appropriate for him or her. Even if a mentally retarded child is fifteen and has a mental age of three, she or he can clean up by putting objects in a pile or basket or can take dishes off a table and leave them on a kitchen counter. If nondisabled siblings see that their brother or sister has a "job," no matter how simple, feelings of unfairness and competition are defused. Sometimes, when it is appropriate, parents need to tell the disabled child in front of the nondisabled children that he or she is wrong and must apologize. This requirement may also help the unaffected siblings see that the disabled child is not wearing the armor of "do-no-wrong."

Praising the Nonhandicapped Siblings' Accomplishments

It is crucial that parents not take the accomplishments of their nonhandicapped children for granted, or these children will grow up feeling that, no matter how much they do, it is not enough to get their parents' praise. Lack of acknowledgment may also lead to resentment when the handicapped child receives tremendous feedback for simple accomplishments, such as writing his or her name or using the potty for the first time. Although it is certainly justified to praise the developmentally disabled child lavishly for doing something that was hard for her or him to learn, parents need to be mindful of how such praise may look to a sibling whose own accomplishment of the same milestone may have been taken in stride. The best compensation is to make an extra effort to find things that the nondisabled child can be praised for frequently.

It is especially vital to praise accomplishments that do and do not pertain to the disabled sibling. The normal siblings can really benefit from receiving positive feedback for just being good: If a six-year-old has been quietly watching a videotape for an hour, coming in and putting the six-year-old on one's lap and giving him or her a completely unsolicited hug for being so quiet and paying such good attention is an important form of praise.

Potentially Embarrassing Situations

When there is a child with a developmental disability in the family, there will be embarrassing moments when the child does something that makes people outside the family stare and feel uncomfortable. Sometimes the parents feel embarrassed, and sometimes the other children do, too. It is not particularly helpful for a parent to imply that being embarrassed is bad (e.g., "What's the matter? Are you ashamed of your brother?"). To feel awkward or embarrassed is a normal reaction to an abnormal situation. In most cases, embarrassment will occur in situations that nobody has control over, and this lack of control will become the focus (e.g., in response to an autistic child's flapping his hands at the beach). One parent noticing the other's annoyance and embarrassment may also feel embarrassed and say, "Well, what do you want me to do about it?" Such a response further confuses the non-disabled siblings, who don't know whether to ally their feelings with the parent who expresses upset, too, or with the parent who is just trying to ignore the incident and convey that feelings about the situation shouldn't matter. It may be that nothing can be immediately done about the embarrassment that the child is causing; however, this doesn't make it any less embarrassing. Sometimes, just making a joke about the child's embarrassing behavior can break tension and create an alliance among all the family members, like saying, "Well, if Billy keeps flapping and pacing up and down along the edge of the water, people are going to think he's a seagull and start feeding him popcorn!" As suggested earlier, humor in a tense situation may be valuable when it benefits other family members, who need to share an acknowledgment that it doesn't feel great to be embarrassed in public.

For siblings in adolescence, the embarrassment factor plays a more central role. Appearances in public and among one's peers are crucial to the adolescent's self-esteem. A child who never noticed or cared about a sibling's awkward public displays before may, around twelve or thirteen, start to protest vehemently about going out in public with a handicapped brother or sister. Here, too, gender and birth order are important. A fourteen-year-old girl will be more concerned about the actions of an eighteen-year-old brother than a fifteen-year-old boy will be about the actions of a four-year-old brother, because the older the disabled sibling gets and the more he or she displays behavior that is not appropriate to age norms, the more uncomfortable the adolescent sibling is likely to feel.

Problem-Solving Skills

Many of the situations that arise in families with disabled children are predictable, and it is important to have a system for handling them. Instituting such a system early will establish healthy habits, will help decrease marital strain, and will create skills that the siblings will take with them into adulthood. Important issues are often emotionally loaded and thereby fertile ground for misunderstanding and communication breakdown. For this reason, a family can benefit from developing a conditioned response of "taking time out" before issues come up so that the crisis can be dealt with rationally. The family needs a prescribed protocol, whether it is dealing with a five-year-old who doesn't want her desk rearranged by her seven-year-old autistic brother, or with a young adult who has returned from college and doesn't want to spend his first Saturday afternoon at home visiting his brother at a group residence.

Better communication between parents and nondisabled siblings consists of a series of steps: (1) expressing and defining the problem; (2) being heard; (3) finding the solution; and (4) carrying out the solution. Below are some examples:

Expressing and Defining the Problem

What seems like the easiest step in problem solving is actually the most crucial and the most difficult. It is important to define the problem in a nonthreatening fashion, articulating it in a way that helps others not to feel defensive. This is a difficult enough task for adults; certainly, in most instances, children do not have the maturity to do this well, if at all. However, parents can work on themselves and can help their children learn how to phrase their needs in a productive way.

In defining a concern or need, it is important to be specific and not to blame. The aim is to be nonconfrontational rather than confrontational. A good technique is to begin a sentence with *I* instead of *you, this,* or *everything.* In this way you make it clear to the listener that you are really talking about yourself and your own feelings. Some examples and counterexamples will help illustrate this point.

These are confrontational approaches to communication:

1. *Wife to husband*: "You don't understand that Bill is impossible to deal with; you need to do more."
2. *Parent to child*: "What do you mean you can't bring friends home? There's nothing to be ashamed of!"
3. *Child to parent*: "Nobody else I know has to leave a restaurant because their brother has a tantrum. I hate him. He's ruining my life!"

These are nonconfrontational alternatives:

1. "Dealing with Bill all day is very taxing. I sometimes feel as if you don't understand the severity of his condition. I would like to have an hour each day when I can be by myself."
2. "I realize that bringing friends home must be difficult and sometimes embarrassing. I am sorry about this. Let's see if there is any way we can help you."
3. "I am upset that we have to leave the restaurant whenever Bill is misbehaving. This doesn't happen to a lot of my friends, and I sometimes wish I was in their family."

Being Heard

The next step, after expressing oneself nonconfrontationally, is being heard. The other members of the family need to listen actively and to repeat what they believe one said, so that there is no misunderstanding. In order to do this one must overcome the natural instinct to become guarded and to defend oneself. The following are some samples of overly defensive responses to the problems articulated in the examples above, followed by more appropriately communicative reformulations:

1. *Defensive*: "What do you mean, I don't understand; of course, I understand. *You* don't understand *me*; I work all day, and I don't have any extra hours to give."

Communicative: "I didn't realize you felt that way. I have a busy schedule and feel pressure too, but let's see what we can do."

2. *Defensive*: "I'm sorry to hear that, but it's just too bad. You'll just have to live with it. What do you want us to do about it? Just be thankful you're not Bill."

   Communicative: "It's OK to have these feelings, and I realize that having Bill in the house can be embarrassing for you when you have friends over. Let's see what we can do about it."

3. *Defensive*: "So this family isn't good enough? No family is perfect. You should be ashamed of yourself."

   Communicative: "What I am hearing you say is that you wish that we could do some things that other families do without difficulty. Let's see if there is a way we can work this out."

Finding the Solution

Having gone through the first two, more difficult stages, finding the solution is actually the fun, creative part. Here, everyone in the family should sit down and list all the possible alternatives, regardless of whether they seem realistic. This may prove to be an opportunity for the family to connect through humor if people generate funny ideas just to lighten things up. Certainly, for a solution to work, the needs of everyone involved must be taken into account. But in order to find that workable solution, the idea here is just to generate a list of ideas. Multiple ideas that could be generated for solving the above conflicts include the following:

1. Mom has an hour each day while Dad stays at home; or a third person is hired to come into the house; or the siblings watch the disabled child; or a friend or relative comes in to help.

2. Friends are invited over at times when the disabled sibling is not at home; or the parents take the disabled sibling out

when the other children have friends come over; or the disabled sibling stays in another part of the house when the siblings have friends over.
3. The family goes out to eat once a week without the disabled sibling; or the family doesn't go out to eat as a whole group but separately with mom or dad.

Carrying Out the Solution

Once the best solution for everyone is decided on, carrying out the plan can be the easier part. It must be kept in mind, however, that a family must be prepared to change the plan with time. Solutions work for a period, and then new conflicts arise. The main point is developing a system for dealing with conflict and feelings. It is this overall skill rather than any particular plan that will come in handy over time.

Aids to Family Coping from Outside the Home

Support Groups

Attending support group meetings may be a very productive activity for all family members, enabling them to see what others have gone through and providing a safe place to air concerns, fears, and feelings of anger. Most of all, attending a support group breaks down feelings of isolation and alienation. And as with education and information, parents who take advantage of support groups themselves are more likely to be in a position to help their nondisabled children understand their own feelings and to find opportunities for opening up family discussion. Attending a support group will bring the nondisabled children into contact with other siblings of a disabled child who are telling their stories and expressing themselves. Children who see others express themselves over time in a group setting may begin to do so themselves.

Most important, nondisabled siblings sometimes feel more comfortable discussing things with sympathetic strangers than with their parents. Overall, attendance at group meetings has been found to facilitate talking in the family setting as well, because siblings will often come home and talk about what they have discussed. They may "enter through the back door" by discussing what someone else in their group has experienced, but they are often looking for an indication that it is OK to begin discussing these issues.

Support Organizations

There are numerous organizations, such as the Association for Retarded Citizens (ARC), the Easter Seal Society, and disorder-specific societies such as the Autism Society of America and the Muscular Dystrophy Association, as well as support-specific groups run through United Way agencies, that can provide families with literature, seminars, and support groups. Another support, which is sometimes available through a diagnostic clinic or treatment program, is parent pairings. A doctor or other professional may (with the appropriate consents) be able to put families with similarly affected children in touch with one another on a one-to-one basis. This contact may be particularly helpful if the families have nonaffected siblings the same age, and if the families live in the same geographic area and can share information about the particular schools and doctors who have been most helpful.

Without accurate information about a child's disorder, and without being in touch with others who are having similar experiences, a family may go off on a tangent of their own and become immersed in their own reasoning about the child's disorder. One example of how lack of information can have a detrimental effect involved a parent who had recently immigrated from Russia. He felt that his autistic son had the potential to get better and/or become normal if only he, as the parent, devoted enough time to the child. The father didn't want to attach the label of autism to his son, especially in front of his other son, who was normal. The father believed that identifying his autistic son as autistic would impede his growth. Therefore, the normal son was led to believe that there was no problem except that his autistic brother's behavior required more parental attention than he himself needed. The father even spent designated "respite" time with his autistic son, giving extra "tutoring." Unfortunately, not only was the autistic son not getting any better, but the other son began wondering what was wrong with him—and why his father spent virtually no time with him. With more support from the educational system and a better understanding of his son's disorder, this father might have been helped to appraise more realistically what was in each son's best interests.

Individual Counseling

Individual counseling is a good complement to a support group. Therapy should be offered to nondisabled siblings as an option if they seem to be having difficulty coping. As we mentioned in Chapter 7, the child who responds to the circumstances of living with a developmentally disabled sibling by withdrawing may be the most in need of individual treatment and may benefit most from an ongoing, individual supportive relationship. Therapy is something that a child should understand and express an interest in; foisting therapy on a child who resists it probably won't help much. Parents also need to be careful in suggesting individual therapy alone when treatment of the whole family is what is really needed. Pushing psychotherapy for a rather normal child may make the child feel that there is something wrong with him or her. There *are* times when a child may need therapy and may actively resist it, but parents should rely on the consultative expertise of experienced therapists in deciding whether to go ahead with therapy. It is really helpful when families can find a therapist who has had experience working with developmentally disabled children, or working with families in similar circumstances.

Residential Placement

> And to David this was the denial of the hope he didn't know
> until that moment he'd still entertained: the hope that his son
> would change. An autistic boy, a beautiful autistic boy, is one
> thing. An autistic man, another. . . . This final crushing aspect
> of bad luck, the accident that was Randall. With shaking
> hands he carefully locked Randall's door again. (Sue Miller,
> *Family Pictures*)

One of the most difficult decisions that a family must face at
the time of the disabled child's adolescence or early adulthood is
whether to place that child in a group home. Perhaps no decision
has more potential for polarizing a family. Making this decision
involves staring the reality of the child's condition in the face. This
process forces the family to tear down the walls of denial; it can no
longer pretend that the disability is not so bad or hold onto the
hope that the child will one day outgrow this condition and become normal. Old wounds are reopened, and the parents may
relive the trauma of discovering they have a less than perfect baby.
This can even occur after years of trying every form of treatment
and attending parent groups and conferences, all with the hope
that some new miracle drug or therapy will come along that will
enable the child to go out on his own. But with the decision to
place the child in the hands of others, this glimmer of hope fades.

I know, from my own experience with my brother, Marc, that
he probably would have done much better had he been placed in
a group home at age thirteen or fourteen. He would have functioned better in the controlled environment that such a home
offers, and it would have engaged him on a level that was virtually
impossible at home. Since his placement in a home, my brother's
speech has improved, and he appears better disciplined. I believe
the reason is that he is not given things unless he pronounces their
names or is behaving somewhat appropriately. The twenty-four-
hour-a-day patience necessary to administer these requirements
with a near-perfect level of consistency is unavailable in the average family. Had Marc been placed earlier, he would have devel-

oped these skills earlier, and the rest of our family would have had more time together. Still, Marc would have been available to us for outings and vacations.

Placement is never an easy decision. It is almost impossible for the immediate family members to objectively assess whether the disabled family member would do better, the same, or worse in a placement outside the home. Most families require compassionate professional help to ease the pain involved and to make the right decision at the right time. Having outside help in making the placement decision can defuse the tensions that may build up among the different opinions of the siblings and the parents.

In most families, all siblings grow up together and reach new stages of development at similar times. The sadness and sense of loss associated with a young adult leaving home for college or marriage or work or travel are tempered by the joy of seeing the child grow. When one member of the family is developmentally disabled, such transition points in the siblings' life cycle are complicated. Siblings who move on are often plagued by "survivor guilt" and other difficult emotions because they have left home for "good" reasons (e.g., to get an education), whereas their disabled sibling has left home for "bad" reasons (e.g., because the parents can no longer cope alone with the burden of care).

Although many people are accustomed to occasionally seeing mentally retarded children about, these children grow up to be adults and, in general, have a full life expectancy, as do the problems and difficulties encountered by the family. They do not end after a family member leaves home. All members of the family remain tied to the disabled relatively emotionally and sometimes, eventually, financially and legally. Unpleasant details, such as what will happen to the disabled child after the parents have died, must eventually be confronted. When discussions of these details take place between parents and adult siblings in the parents' later years, the dialogue may open up old wounds often covered by denial.

Very little has been written about what happens to developmentally disabled children or their families once the children grow up. The family's problems are not fully resolved even if the affected child or adult is placed in a group home. All of the problem-solving skills we have discussed will be needed in terms of estate management and relocation for the parents and the siblings. The parents' retirement plans are frequently altered. Parents who want to be close to all of their children are confronted with a choice, especially if the disabled child has been placed in a group home and can't be easily moved to another because of long waiting lists and state residency requirements. Should the parents leave that child behind and move closer to their other children? How will they process the guilt if they do so? Should siblings take advantage of opportunities to relocate themselves and their new families, or should they stay behind? If they move on, how will *they* process the guilt? The next chapter discusses the practical aspects of being an adult sibling of a developmentally disabled adult. It covers the legal and service aspects of the rights of a disabled sibling and what needs to be done to obtain help for a developmentally disabled adult.

Chapter 11

Legal Aspects of Becoming Your Brother's Keeper

MICHAEL A. ZATOPA, ESQ.

Responsibilities of an Adult Sibling

Many siblings of disabled persons find themselves in the position of becoming responsible for their brother or sister, either because of the early death or disability of their parents, or because of the eventual infirmity or death of their parents later in life. Given your interest in this chapter, you are very likely a sibling of a developmentally disabled person, and either have become or may in the future become responsible for the care and finances of your disabled sibling.

Although you are likely to have become familiar with the problems and stresses of such responsibilities by talking with or observing your parents, it is more often the case that such conversations or observations were quite limited. The legal and financial responsibilities associated with the care of a disabled person are difficult to communicate, but extremely powerful to experience. As a result, it is safe to say that the ramifications of your role will not become apparent until you finally assume the role yourself.

If you have yet to find yourself in the position of caretaker, we can only hope to provide some idea of what will be involved if and when you do assume this role. If you are already in this role, you are far more likely to be motivated to learn about practical suggestions that will simplify this sometimes over- whelming task, not only because of the time involved, but because it is a job that will last the lifetime of your sibling. Even if you do not provide the care in your own home, your monitoring of the financial and service status of your sibling will, even if sporadic, need to be vigilant.

You will find two principal responsibilities in the role of care- taker. The first is to take the proper legal and financial actions to ensure your legal authority to act on your sibling's behalf, as well as to ensure that any financial resources available for your sibling are obtained and preserved. The other is to ensure that your sibling will receive the greatest access possible to the services available, such as a residence, vocational services, and health care. Because most families have nowhere near the resources necessary to provide the tremendously costly services involved, most if not all of the services and finances are obtained through the public sector.

Given the tremendous struggle in our society to define the role of government, it is important that you understand how much this controversy will affect you in your role if you are not able to provide for your sibling financially. Given the cost simply of food, clothing, and shelter, let alone vocational and health services, the vast majority of you will be unable to pay for all of your sibling's needs on your own. Therefore, most if not all of your role will be advocating for your sibling before various public agencies and the courts. In this light, before addressing the specific legal, financial, and service issues you will face, the political and psychological issues involved in obtaining public services will be discussed.

Following a review of the philosophical issues you will face, there will be a practical review, first of the legal and financial issues you will face, and then of the various public programs and services with which you may be involved. Because virtually all of the laws and programs have specific state requirements, even if they are federally mandated. I do not attempt to provide the technical requirements for each program or issue. Rather, I attempt to introduce you to the fairly universal categories of legal issues and programs that involve disabled persons and, most important, to suggest strategies for gaining access to services and programs and obtaining professional assistance and advocacy when you are faced with obstacles.

The Politics and Psychology of Public Services

Everyone knows that life in contemporary society has become more complex, and that much of that complexity has come from the tremendous growth in the law and government. Anyone who pays taxes, gets married, buys a car or a house, or opens a bank account knows how confusing and intimidating the law and government can be.

As the sibling of a disabled person responsible to act on their behalf, you are likely to find the issues and problems of law and government the most frustrating and overwhelming aspect of your role. The primary reason is simple: Seriously disabled persons are unable to generate, through productive employment, enough resources to support themselves. Their very existence, except in the rare instances where the family is extremely wealthy and can support the individual, depends on government programs and financial support. As a result, although the legal and technical issues involved in the responsible sibling's role may be daunting, the emotional and philosophical issues may become more a source of confusion and frustration than understanding the rules that govern various programs.

In order to understand the frequently high emotional pitch involved in dealing with government agencies, I present a general political and social overview of the government programs, in order to provide a context for the divergent views in our society about such programs.

Services for the Disabled and the Tax Revolt

Anyone who has even a vague interest in contemporary politics in the United States, or who is familiar with the phrases "Reagan revolution," "tax revolt," "welfare state," "tax and spend," or "Clintonomics," knows that probably the most controversial issue facing our country is the role of government and the federal budget. Although politics throughout recorded history has debated the role of government in society, the controversy regarding the role of government in the United States has changed substantially as government, beginning in the 1930s and expanding greatly in the 1960s, has become more heavily involved in "social programs," particularly income support, health benefits, pensions and social security, and education. Now, given the high inflation and unemployment rates in the mid-1970s and the huge deficits of the 1980s, the controversy seems to come down to whether these various government programs are part of the cause of, or the solution to, social and economic problems.

While attempting to condense complex social problems into simple dichotomies is as much the problem as anything, for our purposes understanding the two "sides" of the government controversy is important in developing a grasp of the emotional issues that will inevitably arise in seeking government support for a disabled person.

The viewpoint of what is usually termed *conservatism* is based on a philosophy of self-reliance and family independence. The consequence of this philosophy is that individuals and families are responsible for themselves, and that any attempt by government to intervene where the family cannot care for its own members encourages dependency and thereby the breakdown of the family. This viewpoint, in its absolute form, sees the role of government strictly as the protector of competition in the workplace and the provider of police and fire services, and it assumes that current taxing and spending policies for social services are, in fact, the cause of, not the solution to, poverty and welfare dependency. A key belief of conservatism is that individuals are responsible for their own circumstances.

The contrary viewpoint, frequently termed *liberalism*, is that society has a social responsibility to provide services to, and support for, those members of society who, through "no fault of their own," are unable to provide adequate care for themselves. In this viewpoint, there are many causes for families to be unable to provide adequate care to their members, and where causes are beyond the control of those involved, the government should provide various services to prevent poverty or illness. In fact, much of the government bureaucracy exists to determine the degree to which individuals may be to "blame" for their situation, and then to determine the nature and extent of the services to be provided accordingly.

Beginning with the tax revolt in California by the passage of Proposition 13 in 1978 and the Reagan revolution in 1980, there was a clear shift toward the conservative philosophy throughout the country. The most obvious result was a massive reduction in government income, although not necessarily in government spending. It should be noted that, although the philosophical split in political viewpoints is distinct, the public has tended to vote for tax reductions, promoted by conservative forces, but has resisted spending cuts, such as in social security, a liberal position. This contradiction speaks more to human fallibility than to disciplined philosophy, but it goes a long way, in conjunction with the conservative–liberal split, toward explaining why it is so difficult to obtain appropriate services for the disabled.

In essence, most of the liberal programs developed since the New Deal, including social security disability payments, Supplemental Security Income, special-education services, developmental disabilities services, and Medicaid, have remained in law, notwithstanding the conservative trends since 1980. As a result, the increased cost of the bureaucracy's determining who is eligible for services and the increase in the number of persons eligible for services, particularly retired persons, in conjunction with the reduction in rates of taxation, have sharply decreased, per capita, the available funds for these programs.

The net result is simple: *Government bureaucracies simply do not have enough funds to provide all the services they are mandated by law to provide.* A common response of bureaucracy when services are sought for an eligible individual is to use roadblocks that delay or prevent the provision of services. The roadblocks are usually of the following two varieties.

Psychological Barriers

Psychological barriers include a hostile stance by the employees of government agencies, in conjunction with attempts to make people feel guilty for applying for government funds. In essence, the approach is to make it seem that the individual is applying for welfare and should feel guilty for being dependent.

Technical Barriers

Technical barriers involve making the rules and procedures for applying (e.g., forms and eligibility criteria) so complicated and burdensome as to deter as many applicants as possible from completing the application process or from pursuing avenues of appeal if services are denied.

Strategies for Gaining Access to Services

Given the various roadblocks that are frequently faced in gaining access to government programs and legal services for a disabled person, there are several crucial components in a strategy for meeting the needs of that person.

The "Ridiculously Reasonable" Approach

Given the political forces in society noted above, it is important to understand that the roadblocks are caused by social forces, not the personalities of government employees. The plethora of government programs, along with the insufficient tax base to fund them, is a structural problem of government. As a result, all government employees are under pressure, because of inadequate budgets, to create roadblocks to granting services. If the employee does not assume this role, she or he is likely to be out of a job. Most important, these employees are not bad people; they are pressured.

The most important component of a successful strategy is to prevent the development of animosity between you and the government employee. An even better approach is to create a pleasant rapport, as most government employees are treated badly and respond well to courtesy and pleasantness. However, not all employees will respond well, and some will continue to be rude or abusive even after a pleasant approach. That's the reason for the "ridiculously reasonable" strategy. No matter how discourteous (short of assaultive) the employee is, you must be "ridiculously reasonable" in your response. In other words, don't let him or her get to you.

The most important benefit of this approach, aside from the fact that courtesy is always a good policy, is that it prevents a diversion from the true issue of whether your sibling is entitled to the services you are seeking. A hostile relationship with the employee is likely only to increase the chance that you will be denied appropriate services from the agency, as the merits of your claim will be lost in the cross-fire.

Know the Rules

Each one of the financial, service, and legal areas that we discuss here has its own set of complex rules governing how it will affect your life and that of the disabled person. Moreover, these rules have certain "layers" of complexity, the importance of which increases in direct correlation with the cost of the service and the degree to which there is a dispute about eligibility for the service or its nature and extent.

The purpose of the following discussion of the available services and programs is to provide an introduction to the surface layer of rules, that is, the basic nature of the most common programs and services for disabled individuals and their eligibility criteria. However, after the initial contact with the government agencies that provide these services, or the initial application process, it is important to obtain as much understanding as possible of how the specific program operates. Most programs have ongoing requirements and review processes that require a fairly sophisticated understanding of the rules of the game.

Use Professional Help

Given the increasing complexity of the various programs and services available from the government, as well as the financial issues involved in caring for the disabled, it is important (1) to know when it is necessary to use legal and clinical professionals to assist you in obtaining care for your sibling, and (2) to know how to go about attaining the services of professionals with the appropriate expertise. Following a review of the various types of programs, services, and financial issues generally involved in caring for a disabled individual, I discuss in more detail the use of professionals in assisting you with your task.

Legal and Financial Issues

The first and most pressing issues you will address if you become legally responsible for a disabled sibling will be the nature of your legal relationship to your sibling and your financial responsibility for her or him. Although these issues are highly technical, vary considerably from state to state, and require the use of an attorney to resolve successfully, several components of these responsibilities and issues are generally universal and can be summarized.

Conservatorships and Guardianships

Generally, parents retain the authority to make decisions for their children, as well as the financial responsibility to provide for their care, until they reach the age of majority, usually eighteen or twenty-one. On reaching the age of majority, an individual is presumed to possess the faculties to make decisions for themselves, and to meet their own needs for independent living. However, state laws generally provide procedures for determining that an individual who has reached the age of majority is incapable of making some or all of her or his own decisions, and for appointing a person to make decisions on that person's behalf, frequently termed a *conservator* or *guardian*. The procedure may be used exclusively for personal decisions or may involve financial decisions as well.

Personal decision-making authority includes the power to decide on place of residence, consent for medical treatment, the obtaining of public services, voting, or marrying. Financial powers include investment decisions; spending for food, clothing, and shelter; and obtaining professional services.

Once the legal procedure for obtaining the powers described above is completed, the courts generally review the conservatorship or guardianship periodically and, where finances are concerned, require you to submit inventories and accountings of expenditures and assets.

It is strongly recommended that an attorney be consulted for these procedures, as they can be overwhelming for a layperson without advice. Usually, once the procedures are established, only periodic consultation with the attorney will be necessary.

It must also be noted that, in most cases, the law will not mandate that a conservator or guardian be appointed. However, it is *strongly* recommended that, if you desire to act on behalf of or to provide for an adult disabled sibling, an appointment be obtained. It is far too easy for your sibling to be taken advantage of by custodians, or even by government employees desirous of minimizing their responsibilities, if you do not have full legal authority to act on your sibling's behalf.

Wills and Trusts*

In estate planning for the financial security of a disabled son or daughter, parents with modest means are faced with two alternatives, neither of which may be satisfactory. The first alternative is an outright legacy. If the amount bequeathed to the disabled person, however, consists of cash or other nonexempt resources in excess of approximately $2,000 in value, the individual would be rendered ineligible for Supplemental Security income (SSI) and Medicaid (see below). SSI provides a monthly subsistence-level cash grant for food, clothing, and shelter, and Medicaid pays for certain medical expenses.

Unless the legacy is quite large, it is likely to be depleted during the disabled person's life by the high costs of residential care and other specialized services. If this occurs, the individual will be returned to SSI and Medicaid, but with no emergency or supplemental fund to pay for needs that public assistance does not provide, such as dental care, special equipment, and recreation.

A second alternative is to exclude the disabled person from the parents' wills entirely. If other eligibility requirements are satisfied, this exclusion ensures the individual's eligibility for SSI and Medicaid. Disinheritance, however, denies the child protection against unforeseeable events, such as program cutbacks or insolvency. Parents are understandably dubious about entrusting their child's fate to total reliance on public programs for the indigent, considering the shifting winds of politics and the variable national economy.

---

*This section of the chapter was contributed by Sterling Ross, Esq., Mill Valley, California.

The third alternative is a trust. Countable resources for SSI eligibility purposes are defined as cash or other assets that a recipient owns and could convert to cash to be used for support and maintenance. This definition has four requirements, all of which must be satisfied to make an asset a countable resource:

1. The recipient must have an ownership interest in the asset.
2. The individual must be independently able to deal with the property (i.e., it must not be subject to legal dispute, nor should it require the assent of a second person to use, like a joint bank account).
3. The property must be convertible to cash.
4. Though convertible to cash, if the cash won't be usable for food, clothing, and shelter, the property is not a resource of the recipient.

The Social Security Administration (SSA) has developed policy guidelines to assist eligibility workers in determining whether the principal of a trust is a countable resource. Basically, if the beneficiary (the disabled person) has unrestricted access to the principal of the trust, it is counted as a resource. But if a trustee, such as a parent or an adult sibling is given discretion in the use of the trust funds, including being able to use the principal for the support and maintenance of the beneficiary, it is *not* counted as a resource of the disabled person.

Under these guidelines, access to principal is the primary consideration in determining eligibility. If the beneficiary (1) cannot control the amount or frequency of trust distributions and (2) cannot revoke the trust and use the funds for the beneficiary's personal benefit, then the trust principal is not a countable resource.

Some SSA offices are applying an additional requirement: The trust terms must show that the parents (or whoever else may be giving the money to set up the trust) intended that the trust was *not* intended to be the primary source of money for caring for the beneficiary.

The special-needs trust is a type of *discretionary, spendthrift* trust. Its provisions allow the trustee to use either the income or the principal, or both, from the trust for the special needs of the beneficiary. The term *special needs* is defined in the trust as things that are needed to maintain the disabled person's good health, safety, and welfare when, in the discretion of the trustee, such requisites are not being provided by any public agency of any state or of the United States.

Given the complexity of rules about trusts and the importance of following them to prevent the loss of public benefits, it is strongly recommended that your special-needs trust be drafted by an attorney specializing in estate planning.

Supplemental Security Income

SSI is a federal program that provides income assistance to low-income disabled persons. The program is administered by the Social Security Administration (SSA), the same federal agency that administers SSA retirement benefits. Given the nature of autism, mental retardation, and closely related disabilities, virtually all such individuals are eligible for SSI benefits as disabled persons. The only issue is whether a disabled person is "low-income."

Assuming that your sibling has no substantial assets or income of her or his own (see "Wills and Trusts" above), the only issue is residence. If a disabled minor lives with her or his natural or adoptive parents in their residence, their income will be "deemed" to the minor and is likely to prevent eligibility. However, if your sibling is an adult, resides with you as a sibling exclusively, or, as a minor or adult, resides in a publicly supported residential facility or institution, she or he is likely to be eligible for SSI benefits.

Given the relatively straightforward rules for SSI, it is advised that, if your sibling is a minor in a residential facility or school or is an adult, you simply go to the local SSA office and make an application for SSI on your sibling's behalf. Only if you are denied eligibility should you contact a lawyer.

Health Benefits and Medicaid

Medicaid is the medical insurance program operated by the federal government for low-income persons. Simply put, if your sibling is eligible for SSI, she or he will automatically qualify for Medicaid, and in most cases, the converse is true. Medicaid is administered by state and local agencies in each state, and each state has its own laws for complying with federal mandates. Should you have any questions regarding what medical and other health services your sibling may be eligible for under Medicaid, you should first contact your local health department office and, if you remain unsure, contact an attorney.

Public Services for Disabled Persons

Because this book has a national audience, and because all of the services that I discuss here are administered by state and local governments, with varying sets of rules in each state, this review is only a general review of the government programs and the basic parameters of what is available. Some programs are mandated by the federal government and therefore are available to all developmentally disabled persons in all states. Others are administered at the discretion of the states and therefore may or may not be available in your state. These variations are discussed accordingly.

Special-Education Services

A federal law, the Individuals with Disabilities Education Act (IDEA), mandates that all school districts in every state provide a free and appropriate public education for all disabled students regardless of the severity of the disability. The IDEA is designed to ensure that no disabled student will be excluded from an education, and that all will be educated with nondisabled peers to the greatest degree possible. The IDEA also gives the "parents" of each disabled student, who may include guardians or others who are acting as parents (such as responsible siblings), the right to participate in the development of an individualized education program (IEP), and to obtain an impartial determination if the parent disagrees with the education offered by the district. Districts are also obligated to provide all necessary education *and* related services, excluding medical services, *necessary* for the disabled student to be educated, including such services as physical therapy, adapted physical education, behavior training, and even residential services.

Given the scope of this book and the tremendous complexity of the special-education laws and issues, any attempt to give comprehensive information on the IDEA would be ineffective. However, there are strategies for gaining access to information about special-education laws, as well as for approaching special-education issues. These strategies are basically universal. They are discussed, along with strategies for gaining access to other services, below.

Developmental Disabilities Services

Developmental disabilities are generally defined as conditions that arise congenitally or before the age of eighteen; they are expected to be permanent conditions, and they substantially impair a person's ability to live independently. They include conditions such as mental retardation, autism, and cerebral palsy. Given the history in the United States of the institutionalization of the developmentally disabled, the federal Developmental Disabilities Act (DDA) focuses on requiring each state to provide reasonable care to its developmentally disabled, and on preventing the states from mistreating such persons and violating their civil rights. Unfortunately, the U.S. Supreme Court has ruled that unlike the IDEA, the DDA does not *entitle* developmentally disabled persons to services from the states. In effect, this means that, although the DDA gives the developmentally disabled certain rights if state or local governments force them into institutional or other settings, it does not require state or local governments to provide services, such as residential or vocational training services. Only where state law independently requires such services are state and local agencies obligated to provide these services.

For example, California has passed the Lanterman Developmental Disabilities Services Act (LDDSA) to mandate that each developmentally disabled person in California has a *right* to such habilitation services as are necessary for the person to live as independently as possible. The California Supreme Court has interpreted this law to mean that each developmentally disabled person is, on meeting the eligibility criteria, entitled to the services prescribed in the LDDSA, such as residential, respite, vocational training, and other services. However, if your state does not have an equivalent statute, there is no way to obtain such services if state or local agencies simply choose not to assume the physical custody of your sibling.

All states, however, maintain procedures for involuntarily "committing" a developmentally disabled person to a secure setting, should that person pose a danger to himself or to others or, in many states, be unable to meet her or his needs for food, clothing, and shelter. As your sibling may meet one or both of these criteria, you may experience firsthand such involuntary commitment laws and procedures. If your sibling is involuntarily committed to a state residential facility, the federal DDA does provide your sibling with the following rights:

- A nourishing, well-balanced daily diet.
- Appropriate and sufficient medical and dental services.
- To be free of physical or chemical restraint unless absolutely necessary, and to be free of such restraint as a punishment or as a substitute for a habilitation program.
- To receive visits from close relatives at reasonable hours without prior notice.
- To reside in facilities with adequate fire and safety standards, with care appropriate for your sibling, and with programs that provide humane care, are sanitary, and protect his or her rights.

As with special education, the following advocacy strategies will assist you to determine the available developmental disabilities services in your state, as well as the resources for gaining access to the available services.

Strategies for Successful Advocacy

Given the increasing knowledge of the clinical sciences about the nature and treatment of developmental disabilities, as well as the growing complexity of the federal and state laws that address persons with disabilities, it is virtually impossible for any family member to successfully advocate for a disabled child or sibling without using two types of professionals: the legal advocate and the clinical specialist. Short of simply finding out the appropriate state or local agency in your community, requesting help, and accepting whatever response is forthcoming (which, given contemporary public budgets and the recent recession, will frequently result in little, if any, assistance), the assistance of these two kinds of professionals is critical to successful access.

Although the prospect of finding and then retaining one, let alone two, professionals may seem daunting, the good news is that, once this process is completed, its success may last for years with little extra effort. Government tends to maintain the current status of services to any individual, so that, although it may be difficult the first time, once the services are obtained they will frequently continue indefinitely. In addition, if problems arise, these professionals will already be involved in and familiar with the case. Given this encouraging reality, let us review the quite universal strategy for gaining access to public services for the disabled.

The Legal Advocate

The legal advocate is a professional, or even a volunteer, who has developed the knowledge and understanding of both federal laws and the equivalent laws in your state that govern special education, developmental disabilities, and other relevant services. It is important to stress that, although such an advocate may be an attorney, it is not essential, or even important, that the advocate be an attorney. Many parent or disability organizations have staff or volunteers who have become extremely knowledgeable about the legal and service rights of the disabled within the scope of their organizations.

As a result, there are two primary approaches to finding such an advocate. The first involves attorney-referral panels or other attorney organizations. Many state bar organizations have committees for the disabled, and many local bar-referral panels list attorneys who have expertise in disability law. Therefore, in order to find an attorney with the appropriate expertise, you should first call the state and local bar associations for the names of attorneys specializing in disability law. Also, many states have a legal services organization called Protection and Advocacy, which is funded by the federal government under the DDA, and which provides representation for the developmentally disabled. If this organization is not able to provide representation, it is likely to have a referral panel of attorneys and/or advocates.

The second approach to obtaining a legal advocate is through organizations that represent parents or specific disabilities. Most states maintain, particularly on a statewide basis, state or local chapters of organizations such as the Association for Retarded Citizens, the Autism Society of America, the United Cerebral Palsy Association, and the Easter Seal Society, which are excellent sources of expertise on the state laws governing services for the disabled. An advantage of contacting an association that deals with your sibling's particular disability is that it may have direct knowledge of particular appropriate programs in your area. It may also know the names of advocates who have been successful in getting services in those programs for other similarly disabled individuals.

Pragmatically, with both the above approaches, the best start is simply to use the phonebook of the state's largest city and state capital, and to look for some of the above organizations, or others involving the disabled. Usually, if you find one such organization, it will provide referrals to others.

Clinical Experts

The role of the clinical expert is crucial from two perspectives. First, and possibly most important, the clinical expert can provide you with some understanding of the physiological and psychological components of your sibling's disabilities, including diagnostic and treatment information. Access to all the services in the world is meaningless without a clinical understanding of what interventions are likely to be successful, particularly behaviorally and vocationally.

Second, the clinical expert is instrumental in obtaining services from the government. Virtually every attempt to obtain government support for services will hinge on the issue of what services are "necessary" or "appropriate" for the disabled person, and answering these questions requires clinical expertise. Although government agencies usually conduct their own evaluations in determining eligibility for services, the experts in their employ frequently are not objective. Given their employment by an agency that has a financial interest in finding that services are not necessary or appropriate, it is simply good practice to obtain an independent clinical review.

The process of finding such clinical experts, who are usually psychiatrists or psychologists, is often closely linked to the process of finding legal advocates described above. State organizations for parents and the disabled frequently know clinical experts as well. The other source for such professionals is large private, public, or university hospitals in your state or area, particularly if one offers a diagnostic clinic. Simply call the hospital, and ask for referrals for psychiatrists or psychologists who specialize in your sibling's disability. Many times, a clinical expert can refer you to an advocate or attorney, just as an advocate or attorney may be familiar with clinicians with expertise in conducting assessments that address the issues raised by the legal procedures necessary to obtain services.

The Use of the Legal and Clinical Advocates

First, on obtaining a legal advocate, you should inform him or her of the services you are seeking for your sibling, such as residential, medical, or vocational services. Ask for an explanation of eligibility criteria for the services you are seeking, as well as the procedure for application and eligibility, including timelines, eligibility criteria, and answers to any other questions you may have. When you meet with a legal advocate, you should come prepared with a list of questions to make sure you get a chance to raise all your concerns, note the answers, and make a list of what you and/or the advocate will need to do next.

Once you understand the procedure for obtaining the services you are seeking, have the legal advocate talk to the clinical professional regarding the legal criteria for your sibling to obtain such services. The timing of the independent clinical expert, preferably before the evaluation by the government agency, is crucial, as is the legal and clinical professionals' discussing the case before the evaluation takes place. The clinical expert must be aware of the appropriate legal questions in order to answer them properly in the report that will be drafted as a result of the evaluation. In most instances, it is recommended that the evaluation by your clinical expert be done before any evaluation by the government. A government agency is more likely to make decisions in your favor if, when it goes through its application process, it has a high-quality evaluation in its hands, which will frequently keep it honest.

The specific issues you will face in your case will be as unique as your sibling. However, there are facets of acting as your brother's keeper that are common to all those in your situation, in particular the direct correlation between your understanding of your rights and the likelihood that you will be successful in your role. Knowing your rights and your sibling's rights, or using the services of an attorney or legal advocate who is a strong advocate on your and your sibling's behalf, is critical in obtaining the best care, and also in creating peace of mind for you (and for your parents if you are acting on their behalf).

I strongly recommend that you use legal and clinical professionals to assist you in your role. Although you will incur some "front-end" costs, obtaining not only adequate services but clinically appropriate services is, without question, the most financially and psychologically cost-effective action you can take on your sibling's behalf.

Afterword

In this book, we have tried to give the reader a sense of what goes on in families with developmentally disabled children. We began with a first-person account of having grown up with an autistic brother. Another perspective we have taken is to explain what scientifically planned research studies have shown about families with a developmentally disabled member. Although such research has been limited and often focuses on basic demographic differences, it reveals some basic trends in the typical patterns of adaptation. It is clear that more such research, especially on psychological processes, is very much needed. Much of what we have presented is based on the clinical experience of working with and talking to many families with developmentally disabled children. The breadth and texture of the experience of many individuals conveys yet another type of portrait of families with developmentally disabled children. However, there is always a danger of wrongly generalizing principles of behavior from individual clinical observations because particularly touching experiences tend to be weighed more heavily than the more common, mundane ones. As a final chapter, we included the perspective of an attorney who has worked with many families like the ones discussed in this book because we felt it was also important for a sibling to have hands-on facts about continuing to cope adaptively with the lifelong problems of being "your brother's keeper." We hope our readers have gained a fuller understanding of the issues we've undertaken to cover through the use of the various perspectives we've included.

In real life, no one individual or family is prototypical, even though we have focused on the prototypical ways in which siblings cope, and on the prototypical family conflicts that arise. In real life, every individual, every family, and every situation form a cross section of the points we have discussed. In the appendixes that follow are materials designed to further personalize the information in this book. We hope this book will be helpful not just to adult siblings trying to better understand their childhood experiences, but also to the generation of parents currently enmeshed in raising disabled and nondisabled brothers and sisters together. As a Japanese proverb says: Life is a long road down which we carry a heavy burden. We wish our readers strength in carrying their burdens.

Appendixes

Discussion-Group and Support-Group Materials and Topics for Individual Consideration

The appendixes parallel topics covered in the text. The material in the appendixes is intended to give readers a structure for relating their specific experiences to the material in the book. Individuals who are trying to better understand their past can use many of these exercises either by writing out responses, or by creating a journal or daily diary that monitors some of these issues as they arise. The various exercises and questionnaires can also be used for discussion topics in support groups. Many of the exercises are also intended to be helpful to therapists who are treating the siblings or parents of a developmentally disabled child in individual or family therapy.

Appendix IA

The Mix of Coping Styles
Adult Siblings—Individual or Group Exercise

You may find it helpful to begin by thinking back to the discussions of the prototypical forms of sibling coping: the parentified child, the withdrawn child, the acting-out child, and the super-achieving child. Although most siblings will see aspects of themselves in one or more of these descriptions, focus on what "percentage mix" you feel you were of these different prototypes at different stages of your growing-up period. With this mix in mind, it should be easier to analyze which things bothered you most and how those negative events affected your mode of adaptation (i.e., your prototype). Then, returning in your thoughts to the present time, you may be more able to think about how your chosen mode of adaptation affects how you respond to caregiving and other close relationships now. Thinking about how you adapted then may also help you to understand the characteristic ways in which you currently cope well or poorly with stress.

Definitions

Parentified: Acting as if in a parenting role, taking responsibility and helping with your sibling above and beyond what most children your own age did with theirs.

Withdrawn: Acting and feeling as if you lived a life that was separate from the rest of the family; feeling as if you didn't matter as much as your disabled sibling.

Acting out: Doing bad things to get back at your parents for their lack of attention for their placing on you too great a burden of care for your sibling, or for your feeling that they really didn't notice or care what you did.

Superachieving: Working very hard to be perfect in school or in a competitive activity; wanting to show that you could make up for or do everything that your disabled sibling could not do.

MODE-OF-COPING MATRIX

% you were each of these:	A parentified child	A withdrawn child	An acting-out child	A superachieving child
Under 5 years old				
6–12 years old				
Adolescent				

Appendix IB

Positive and Negative Connotations of Coping Styles
Adult Siblings—Group Discussion

1. It may be helpful to go through each prototype of sibling coping systematically and for each member in turn to discuss the extent to which he or she relied on each method of coping. This discussion should encourage participation and help deemphasize the "goodness" or "badness" of different prototypes. One or two prototypes may be enough for a one-hour group if everyone takes a turn.
2. Alternatively, a single participant may volunteer to discuss his or her memories about a particular prototype that strongly characterized himself or herself or another sibling. (A sibling may be easier to discuss when the group is new.)
3. Writing each prototype on a piece of paper and having the group members draw them randomly may be a more comfortable approach for other groups. In a more brief time frame, this approach may elicit some discussion of each prototype and, again, prevents individuals' feeling singled out by strong group feelings about one prototype.

Appendix IC

Sibling Areas of Conflict
Adult Siblings—Questionnaire

If you are self-administering these questions, try writing out your answers. Writing may focus your attention on certain issues, and you may then prioritize issues differently from when you merely think about them. Be completely honest with yourself. Distinguish between what you are/were supposed to think and feel and what you really feel. Try to identify where your anger or sadness may come from and who you feel is responsible for your having those feelings.

If you feel comfortable doing so, try these questions out on your other nonhandicapped siblings and even on your parents. Use the information to clarify any misperceptions that you may have of their attitudes toward your disabled sibling, and toward *you* in relation to your disabled sibling. It may also help to discuss your responses with a friend or relative who was close to your family when you were growing up so that you can compare your memories and understanding of events to someone else's.

An individual therapist may use these questions as a pretreatment questionnaire to get an idea of which topics raise the most problems and what kind of a characteristic defense style the client or patient uses.

Specific Issues Questions

Which of these items were a problem for you? How old were you when you first started to feel bad about this item? Write down some key events that you remember and why these memories are particularly strong.

1. *Privacy*: Did you ever feel that your private and personal space was violated without your expecting it to be (or without satisfactory recourse)? Was it hard for you to be alone or to do something alone when you wanted not to be interrupted or bothered?

2. *Personal possessions*: Did you ever have to deal with the destruction of your personal possessions? Do you feel that more could have been done about it by your parents? Did you ever worry about your sibling's harming a family pet that you loved?

3. *Activity level*: Did you ever have difficulty coping with physical hyperactivity, particularly hyperactivity that encroached on your own activities (like ruining something you were building, a game you were playing, or your homework)? Or

did your sibling have uncontrolled motor movements that resulted in problems for you, even though you were told your sibling couldn't control herself or himself any better? Were there things you think your brother or sister might have been taught to control and wasn't? Do you feel different if you think about whether your sibling's behavior was something she or he might have been able to control?

4. *Aggressiveness*: Was your sibling ever physically aggressive to you, your friends, your other siblings, or your parents? How did this aggressiveness make you feel? What was your understanding about how in control or out-of-control your sibling was in his or her aggressiveness? What rules did you have to follow about retaliation? Do you think they were fair rules? Did you ever really hurt your sibling? How intentional were your actions? How did you feel afterward?

5. *Noncompliance*: Were you ever bothered by your sibling's noncompliance? Do you feel you could tell the difference between when he or she didn't understand and when he or she simply didn't follow directions? Did it bother you if your sibling needed things repeated often? What was irritating about this

need for repetition? Did you ever get directly or indirectly punished for your sibling's noncompliance? How did you feel?

6. *Running away:* Did your sibling run away? Were you afraid something might happen to him or her? Were you ever or usually responsible for keeping him or her away from physical harm when you were out in public?

7. *Public embarrassment:* Were you ever made to feel uncomfortable, embarrassed, or angry by the looks or comments of other people about your brother's or sister's appearance or behavior? What did you imagine when you heard unkind things being said? What did the behavior of other people make you want to do? Did your feelings make you want to take action or withdraw?

8. *Home safety*: Were you responsible for keeping your brother or sister from doing unsafe things at home while your parents did other things? Do you feel that you were ever given not enough or too much responsibility? At the time, did you choose to take responsibility? How important was it to your parents that you watch out for your brother or sister? Did you ever fail to do your job so that some major injury befell your sibling? How did you feel about having so much responsibility then? Now?

9. *Talking/interrupting*: Did your brother or sister ever interrupt while you were talking or listening, in order to say something different that interested him or her? How was this interruption handled by your parents? Did you feel it was handled fairly? How did you feel when you couldn't finish what you were talking about with your mother or father because of your sibling? At the time, did you believe that your sibling knew that he or she was interrupting, and that interrupting was not polite?

10. *Competing for parental attention*: Do you remember ever having been physically displaced by your sibling (like getting out of your mother's lap during a story) because he or she wanted

your place? Do you feel you had to make more compromises of this sort than you would have if your sibling had not had a disability? At the time, what was your understanding about having to compromise?

11. *Self-centeredness*: Did your sibling seem excessively self-centered and concerned only with getting things for himself or herself? Did your sibling's acting self-centeredly and demanding ever make you feel that he or she cared about you less than you had thought?

12. *Irritability*: Was your sibling often irritable so that you had to walk on tiptoes not to set him or her off? Did you have to do or not do special things when around him or her to make sure you didn't physically harm him or her with normal behavior like hugging, because he or she was so medically fragile? How did you feel if you accidentally set him or her off anyway? Did you ever do things on purpose to irritate or frighten him or her?

13. *Teacher role*: Were you seen by other family members as your sibling's teacher? Did your parents ever make you feel that you could get your brother or sister to talk or to do other things better than they could? Did this make you feel good, or did this make you feel anxious, or both?

14. *Best friends*: Did your parents ever tell you that you were your sibling's best friend? If they did, did you think it was true? Did you feel that your sibling did, in fact, regard you as his or her best friend? Did you worry about your sibling's feeling jealous or left out if you had a friend your own age over and you did things your sibling didn't understand?

15. *Friendships*: Were you ever uncomfortable having friends over? Did you have them anyway? What did you tell them about your disabled sibling? Did you ever lose friends or end friendships because of how you knew or suspected they felt about your sibling? Did you ever feel you were less popular in school because you had a handicapped brother or sister? Did you ever feel that friends said things behind your back about

him or her? How did you react if someone called your sibling a "retard" or used some other epithet?

16. *Feelings about the cause*: How old do you remember being when you realized your sibling had a developmental handicap? How old were you when you realized it was a lifelong handicap? Did you ever fear that something you yourself had done had caused your brother's or sister's handicap? If you did, did you ever tell anyone else about your fear?

17. *Feeling loved*: Did you ever worry about whether your brother or sister really loved you or not? Did he or she sometimes do things that made you question whether he or she really cared? Did you ever feel angry or cheated by having a disabled sibling instead of a normal one? Whom did you feel angry at?

18. *Being afraid or unsure of your feelings*: Were you ever afraid to talk about how you really felt about your brother or sister? Did you ever feel strongly ambivalent about him or her (i.e., loving and protective at one moment and angry and rejecting at another)? Was it OK in your family to openly express frustration or anger about your sibling's disability? Have you ever looked back and wondered how you really felt about your sibling, as opposed to what you were *told* you felt about your sibling?

19. *Parenting*: Looking back, do you feel that having a disabled sibling changed how your parents raised you? How do you feel that you (or they) would be different today if it hadn't been for your handicapped sibling?

Appendix II

Social Support and Family Resources Questionnaire
Adult Siblings or Parents—
Individual and Group Exercise

In Chapters 3, 4, and 10, we discussed a number of ways in which circumstances within the family and circumstances around the family may contribute to how well a family is able to cope with raising a disabled child. There are no absolute rules about whether the presence or absence of any particular form of social support is pivotal, but in some families, one or two events, persons, or periods of time may mark when a family's ability to cope improved or deteriorated substantially. The following questionnaire will allow you to assess these risk and protective factors on a personal level.

If you grew up with a handicapped sibling, you may want to fix a particular time in your childhood in your mind in order to respond to the questions. It may be equally informative to try to fill out the questionnaire for multiple points in time, including the present. Many families perceive critical changes in social support only when the handicapped child is born or diagnosed, when other sibs are born, when the handicapped sibling entered an out-of-home placement for the first time, or when the nonaffected siblings have all left home.

Similarly, if you are the parent of or other care provider for a handicapped person, you may want to look back at different turning points in your family life and try to recognize when stress or protective factors were peaking and ebbing. You may gain a more integrated perspective by comparing your questionnaire responses, in terms of overall stress levels, with how you imagine your nonaffected children might respond.

The purpose of the questionnaire is to assist you in organizing your personal perspective on the presence or absence of family and social support, and to serve as a means of focusing on issues that up to now may have been less explicitly defined for you.

SOCIAL SUPPORTS FOR FAMILIES WITH DEVELOPMENTALLY DISABLED CHILDREN

	How much impact did this have on you?		
	Positive	No impact	Negative
Question	N/A 1	2 3	4 5
Part 1: Stress and coping factors related to your parents' relationship			
1. The way your parents got along, not involving the children.			
2. The way your parents got along, relating to your sibling.			
3. The way your parents got along, relating to you.			
4. A sense that your mother cared about your sibling more than your father did.			

Question	How much impact did this have on you?				
	Positive		No impact		Negative
	N/A 1		2 3		4 5
5. A sense that your father cared about your sibling more than your mother did.					
6. A sense that your parent(s) wanted you to take sides about things your sibling did or didn't do.					
7. A feeling that your parents split up mainly because of your sibling.					
8. The way you felt your parents usually acted toward your sibling.					
9. The value you felt your parents placed on doing things together as a family.					
10. The value you felt your parents placed on doing things alone with you.					
Part 2: Stress and coping factors related to social support from relatives					
1. Extended family who lived with you.					
2. Extended family whose house you could go to on your own.					
3. Relatives who invited you on family outings that your own family couldn't attend.					
4. Relatives who seemed to imply that your sibling was your parents' "fault."					

Question	Positive	No impact	Negative
	N/A 1	2 3	4 5
5. Relatives who seemed to blame the other side of your family for your sibling's problems.			
6. Relatives who told you they felt sorry for you.			
7. Cousins who were surrogate "normal" siblings for you.			
8. Cousins who made fun of your sibling.			
9. A grandparent who made you feel as if you were the best grandchild.			
10. Relatives who babysat or stayed on weekends so your parents could get away.			
11. Relatives who encouraged you to pretend you were part of their family.			
Part 3: Stress and coping factors related to family economic stability			
1. Your parents would tell you they couldn't afford something you wanted because they had to pay for your sibling's therapy.			
2. Your mother or father complained about limited work choices because of your sibling.			

How much impact did this have on you?

	How much impact did this have on you?				
			No		
	Positive		impact		Negative
Question	N/A	1	2	3	4	5
3. Your parents could afford help, tutors, and special schools.						
4. You had to share a room with your sibling because your parents couldn't afford a bigger home.						
Part 4: Stress and coping factors related to cultural and religious background						
1. In your religion, you were taught that a handicapped child was a special gift from God.						
2. In your religion or culture, a handicapped child was a sign of shame.						
3. Your religious community helped your parents in concrete ways (like baby-sitting or scholarships for you or your sibling).						
4. In your religion or culture, you were brought up to feel that someday you and your other siblings would be expected to care for your disabled sibling.						

	How much impact did this have on you?			
	Positive	No impact	Negative
Question	N/A 1	2 3	4 5
Part 5: Support from professionals			
1. You remember certain teachers who really made a difference for your sibling.			
2. You would be afraid to go to the doctor's if the appointment was to find out about your sibling's problems.			
3. You had a teacher you secretly wished was your mother.			
4. You remember your parents' being sad or angry because doctors couldn't be of more help.			
5. You wanted to become a doctor or a teacher so you could do a better job helping people like your sibling.			

Appendix III

Defenses and Negative Affects
Adult Siblings—
Group or Individual Exercise

This exercise confronts some of the negative feelings that may be associated with growing up with a disabled sibling.

1. Try to identify some of the ways in which your sibling has had a negative impact on your family.

2. What about your life as an adult?

3. Do these ideas come easily to you?

4. Do you feel guilt in thinking about these issues?

5. Does a voice inside you say that you "shouldn't" feel this way?

6. Do you find yourself immediately countering with ways in which your family has been positively affected?

This exercise is designed to help identify ways that people shield themselves from painful emotional realities. Taking into consideration the answers given above, can you identify situations where you may still act in these defensive ways when you encounter painful emotional realities in your life now? If you feel you have overcome some of these difficulties can you identify what has helped you?

Appendix IVA

Adult Siblings
Parentified Child—Questionnaire

This questionnaire is for use in an adult siblings group or as an individual exercise and includes a section on page 254 that parents can complete. This questionnaire corresponds to the material in Chapter 6 "The Parentified Child." For each question, consider the possible pros and cons.

1. How strongly do you identify with the prototype of the parentified child?

2. Does the description of the parentified child in Chapter 6 describe you and your role in your family in the past or present?

3. Does it describe what you were like during a part of your life?

4. Did things change once you reached adolescence?

5. In what ways did your sibling influence your career decision?

6. Are you happy with this decision?

7. While you were growing up, in what way were family outings affected by your sibling?

8. In what way was your interaction with your friends influenced by the presence of your sibling?

9. In what way is your present family affected by your sibling?

10. Do you feel that you are more uncomfortable than others when you are not in control of situations?

11. Do you feel the need to "be helpful" in order to be in control of a situation?

12. Do you choose relationships with people who are needy? Are you more comfortable around such people?

13. Do you check with yourself first or with others when determining whether something "feels right"?

14. When you feel "put out" or taken advantage of, do you suppress your anger?

15. Do you feel you are more of a people pleaser than other people usually are? (List some areas in your life where this is the case, e.g., with friends, coworkers, and family.)

Complete the following sentences:

Adult Siblings

1. As a result of having to look after my sibling, I didn't have time for

2. Because of my sibling, I missed out on

3. Writing about or discussing this topic makes me feel

4. It is difficult for me even to talk about these feelings because there is a voice inside me that says

5. A healthy response to these voices would be

Questions for Parents

1. Take a close look at your family. Is there one child who tends to take more care of the disabled child?

2. Has that child ever complained? If so, describe the interaction:

3. If that child were to complain or be reluctant, what might be your response?

4. Is there any way you can limit the child-care responsibilities of this child?

Parents may also find it helpful to go through the Adult Sibling part of this questionnaire and consider how each of their non-disabled children might answer the questions.

Appendix IVB

Adult Siblings
Withdrawn Child—Questionnaire

This questionnaire is for use in an adult siblings group or as an individual exercise and includes a section that parents can complete. The questionnaire corresponds to the material in Chapter 7, "The Withdrawn Child." For each question consider the possible pros and cons.

Questions for Adult Siblings

1. Do you feel you were a withdrawn child during a part of your life?

2. Did your role change when you reached adolescence?

3. Did you have a lot of friends as a child?

4. Were you reluctant to bring friends home because of the presence of your sibling?

5. Were you reluctant to engage in activities with other children because of embarrassment?

6. In what ways do you feel your personality was shaped by your sibling?

7. In what way did your sibling affect your major life decisions (e.g., choice of college, relocation)?

8. Do you feel very uncomfortable in social situations?

9. Do you tend to withdraw when faced with conflict or difficulty?

10. Would you like to reach out to others but do you find that you can't?

Complete the following sentences:

1. As a result of my disabled sibling, I was unable to

2. While reading the chapter in this book on the withdrawn child, I was feeling

Questions for Parents

1. Take a close look at your family. Is there one child who tends to keep away from family activity, especially when faced with conflict?

2. What happens when you try to engage this child in activity? What is his or her response?

Parents may also find it helpful to go through the Adult Sibling part of this questionnaire and consider how each of their non-disabled children might answer the questions.

Some Suggestions for Parents in Engaging Their Nonhandicapped Children

1. Attempt to connect with them through activities appropriate to their age (e.g., drawings and stories for young children; attending sporting events or movies with older children).
2. Encourage them to join a sibling support group. Speak with them about the feelings and thoughts of other members of the group. Their comments may provide some insight into what they themselves are feeling even if it is difficult for them to share their own feelings.
3. Set family and individual time aside for them. Engage them in activities that have nothing to do with the disabled sibling.

Appendix IVC

Adult Siblings
Acting-Out Child—Questionnaire

This questionnaire is for use in an adult siblings group or as an individual exercise and includes a section that parents can complete. The questionnaire corresponds to the material in Chapter 8, "The Acting-Out Child." For each question, consider the possible pros and cons.

Questions for Adult Siblings

1. Does the description of the acting-out child apply to how you dealt with things as a child?

2. Do you still tend to act out or get angry now when faced with difficulty and conflict?

3. Did the acting-out role you played in your family change with adolescence?

4. If you no longer act out, when did you begin to change?

5. Do you have difficulty dealing with authority figures?

Questions for Parents

1. Take a close look at your family. Is there one child who is acting out to get attention?

2. How do you deal with this acting-out behavior?

3. Are the feelings behind the actions valid?

Suggestions for Parents

1. Try to see where the anger and hostility of the acting-out child is coming from, and try to understand the feelings behind the behavior.

2. Ask the child if anything is upsetting him (or her), rather than assuming that the cause is obvious.

3. Honestly try to note any similarities between the way your child acts and the way you sometimes feel.

4. Suggest to the child alternative ways of dealing with her or his feelings that are more direct, but not harmful to others.

5. Try to engage the child in activities that don't involve the disabled child, and provide opportunities to express aggression.

Appendix IVD

Adult Siblings
Superachieving Child—Questionnaire

This questionnaire is for use in an adult siblings group or as an individual exercise and includes a section that parents can complete. The questionnaire corresponds to the material in Chapter 9, "The Superachieving Child." For each question, consider the possible pros and cons.

Exercises and Questions

1. How strongly do you identify with the prototype of the superachieving child?

2. What was your special role in the family as the superachiever?

3. At what stage did you become seen as the superachiever?

4. Were you reluctant to bring friends home because you were embarrassed?

5. How important to you was attaining your parents' praise?

6. How relatively important to you was praise from key people outside the family (e.g., a teacher, a coach, or an extended family member)?

7. Were your successes taken for granted in your family?

8. Did you find yourself feeling good about what you had done?

9. Did your role and attitude toward the meaning of being successful change in adolescence?

10. Did your role in the family affect your career decision?

11. Does "being a superachiever" describe you today?

12. If not, when did you change?

13. Would you consider yourself a driven person?

14. Do you feel it necessary to achieve in order to feel good about yourself?

15. Do you tend to bury yourself in work during troubling times and times of conflict?

16. Do you ever feel that you have "arrived" after completing a project, or are you immediately off to the next project?

Healing for Superachieving Adult Siblings

If you played and are playing the role of superachiever, there is no need to let go of your achievement motivation in order to heal or to deal with responsibility. However, there are things you can do, beginning with learning to enjoy your successes:

1. The next time you've done something right, tell yourself. Write it down, think about it, and reward yourself by taking some time out to reflect on it. This may sound simple, even childish, but it is recognition that you probably never actually got as a child, so you can give it to yourself now, and you should: You deserve it.
2. Think about what your latest accomplishment means to *you*— not to your family or to society. Make a list if necessary.
3. Are you motivated by internalized "shoulds"? If you are, reconsider. Who *really* says you should, and why? Distinguish what you really want for yourself from what you feel you may be doing for others.

Questions for Parents of Superachievers

1. Take a close look at your family. Is there one child who is the superachiever? Is there too much pressure on her or him?
2. Do you feel that your attention and approval expressed directly to that child are conditional on her or his successes?

Suggestions for Parents of Superachievers

1. Attempt to connect with your superachieving child through activities that are not related to school and/or achievement.
2. Talk about the child's feelings and interests. Try to help him or her distinguish between what he or she is doing for your approval and what he or she truly enjoys doing.
3. Pay particular attention to this child, and give him or her support even, or especially, when he or she is not successful.

Appendix V

Parent–Sibling Interaction
Parent Exercise

Some Suggestions for Parents Regarding Their Nonhandicapped Children

In the context of a parent support group, each of the following suggestions could be raised as a topic. Each may be discussed in terms of ideas that some parents already do or could do to implement them in their own families.

1. Praise their accomplishments, at least once a day.
2. Require the disabled sibling to do as much for herself or himself as possible. (This may be difficult, but it will be helpful to the nondisabled children. The disabled child may learn to use her or his disability to get away with not doing certain tasks.)
3. Encourage the nonhandicapped sibling(s) to join a sibling support group. Make time to discuss what they've heard and felt.
4. Don't force the disabled child on other siblings for babysitting or play if there is no reward for them.
5. Recognize the other siblings' need to be alone with friends without the responsibility of looking after their disabled sibling.
6. Take advantage of respite care to spend time alone with your other children.

Appendix VI

Children's Concept of Developmental Disabilities
Parent Exercise

The following questions can be used as an exercise to gain some insight into your child's level of understanding of developmental disabilities. These discussion topics may also be helpful in drawing your child into discussing his or her own concerns.

1. Do you think your brother or sister is different from other little kids of the same age? (Alternatively, contrast the disabled child with another specific child of the same age whom the sibling knows.)

2. How do you think your brother or sister is different? (Note any focus on physical as opposed to behavioral features.)

3. Why do you think your brother or sister is different? (This is an opportunity to explore whether the child has a sense of personal culpability for his or her sibling's difficulties.)

4. What do you think is wrong with your brother or sister? (It's OK to signal your acknowledgment that something *is* wrong.)

5. Do you think you can catch what your brother or sister has? Does this possibility make you scared?

6. Do you think there is medicine that can make him or her better? How else do you think we might "fix" him? (Use this opportunity to explain how special attention and activities can be like "medicine.")

7. When taking the developmentally disabled sibling to see the doctor, or in other situations where there are likely to be other siblings of developmentally disabled children around, try saying something such as, "That girl is here with her brother, too. I wonder what she is thinking?"

Appendix VII

Family Problem-Solving Approaches
Siblings and Parents—
Home or Family Therapy Exercise

In Chapter 10, we discussed nonconfrontational approaches to family problem solving. By means of the approach modeled in Chapter 10, the following exercises may be tried by all family members as a group:

1. List five common problems and conflicts that your family deals with over and over.

a.

b.

c.

d.

e.

2. Take one of these issues and write a carefully worded statement about it that you can read to another family member so that what you say sounds as nonconfrontational as possible.

3. As you listen to another family member's statement being read, think of responses that you can make that say you are hearing him or her and want to help to find a solution that you can both live with.
4. *Parents*: Think of some of the unspoken difficulties you or your spouse may be having or may have expressed in the past about the developmentally disabled child. Use the techniques in A and B above.

For Further Reading

The following are selected books and specific articles that are central to the research and ideas that informed this book. Most of the books are written for a nontechnical audience and would be good follow-up reading for any reader of this book. The journal articles, chapters, and a few books are a sampling of the technical and more scientific research in this area and are listed here for the interested student in this area who may wish to gain further knowledge of the research.

Books on Siblings of Developmentally Disabled Children

Lobato, D. (1990). *Brothers, Sisters, and Special Needs*. Baltimore: Paul H. Brookes.
  This book gives an overview of sibling relationships and siblings in the context of their families. It provides very detailed and creative materials for conducting support groups for younger siblings.

Powell, T. H., and Ogle, P. A. (1985). *Brothers and Sisters: A Special Part of Exceptional Families*. Baltimore: Paul H. Brookes.
  This book is a great resource for professionals working with families with exceptional children. It includes lots of active advice and is an excellent resource for more interested parents and adult siblings, too.

Stoneman, Z., and Berman, P. W. (1993). *The Effects of Mental Retardation, Disability, and Illness on Sibling Relationships*. Baltimore: Paul H. Brookes.
  This book gives an exceedingly comprehensive summary of the research on siblings of the developmentally disabled, with chapters by

leading researchers. It is the single best starting point for the advanced student wanting an introduction to research in this area.

Popular Books on Related Topics

Brown, E. M. (1989). *My Parents' Keeper: Adult Children of the Emotionally Disturbed.* Berkeley, CA: New Harbinger.

Featherstone, H. (1988). *A Difference in the Family: Living with a Disabled Child.* New York: Penguin.

Goldfarb, Lori. (1986). *Meeting the Challenge of Disability or Chronic Illness: A Family Guide.* Baltimore: Paul H. Brookes.

Gravitz, H., and Bowden, J. (1985). *Recovery: A Guide for Adult Children of Alcoholics.* New York: Simon & Schuster.

McConnel, P. (1986). *A Workbook for Healing: Adult Children of Alcoholics.* New York: Harper & Row.

Miller, S. (1989). *Family Pictures.* New York: HarperCollins.

Schiff, H. S. (1977). *The Bereaved Parent.* New York: Crown.

Singer, S., George, H. S., and Irvin, L. K. (1989). *Support for Caregiving Families: Enabling Positive Adaptation to Disability.* Baltimore: Paul H. Brookes.

Thompson, M. D., and Charlotte, E. (1986). *Raising a Handicapped Child: A Helpful Guide for Parents of the Physically Disabled.* New York: William Morrow.

Technical Journal Articles, Chapters, and Books

Abramovitch, R., Stanhope, L., Pepler, D., and Corter, C. (1987). "The influence of Downs Syndrome on sibling interaction." *Journal of Child Psychology and Psychiatry, 28,* 865–879.

Bibace, R., and Walsh, M. (1980). "Development of children's concept of illness." *Pediatrics, 66,* 912–917.

Blum, M., and William, R. (Eds.). (1991). "Vulnerability and resilience of children and their families." *Pediatric Annals, 20,* 9.

Breslau, N. (1982). "Siblings of disabled children: Birth order and age-spacing effects." *Journal of Abnormal Child Psychology, 10,* 85–96.

Breslau, N., Weitzman, M., and Messenger, K. (1981). "Psychological functioning of siblings of disabled children." *Pediatrics, 67,* 344–353.

Burbach, D. J., and Peterson, L. (1986). "Children's concepts of physical illness: A review and critique of the cognitive-developmental literature." *Health Psychology, 5,* 307–325.

Daniels, D., Moos, R., Billings, A., and Miller, J. (1986). "Psychosocial risk and resistance factors among children with chronic illness, healthy siblings and healthy controls." *Journal of Abnormal Child Psychology, 15,* 295–308.

Dunn, J. (1985). *Brothers and Sisters.* Cambridge: Harvard University Press.

Dyson, L. (1989). "Adjustment of siblings of handicapped children: A comparison." *Journal of Pediatric Psychology, 14*(2), 215–229.

Gath, A. (1974). "Siblings' reactions to mental handicap: A comparison of brothers and sisters of mongol children." *15,* 187–198.

Gath, A., and Gumley, D. (1987). "Retarded children and their siblings." *Journal of Child Psychology and Psychiatry, 28,* 715–730.

Grossman, F. K. (1972). *Brothers and Sisters of Retarded Children.* Syracuse, NY: Syracuse University Press.

Holroyd, J. (1974). "The Questionnaire on Resources and Stress: An instrument to measure family response to a handicapped family member." *Journal of Community Psychology, 2,* 92–94.

Jones, E. D., and Payne, J. S. (1986). "Definition and prevalence." In J. R. Patton, J. S. Payne, and M. Beirne-Smith (Eds.), *Mental Retardation* (2nd Ed.). Columbus, OH: Charles E. Merrill.

Kazak, A. E., and Clark, M. W. (1986). "Stress in families of children with myelomeningocele." *Developmental Medicine and Child Neurology, 28,* 220–228.

Lobato, D., Barbour, L., Hall, L. J., and Miller, C. T. (1987). "Psychosocial characteristics of preschool siblings of handicapped and non-handicapped children." *Journal of Abnormal Child Psychology, 15,* 329–338.

Perrin, E. C., and Gerrity, P. S. (1981). "There's a demon in your belly: Children's understanding of illness." *Pediatrics, 67,* 841–849.

Potter, P. C., and Roberts, M. C. (1984). "Children's perceptions of chronic illness: The roles of disease symptoms, cognitive development, and information." *Journal of Pediatric Psychology, 9,* 13–27.

Schopler, E., and Mesibov, G. B. (Eds.). (1984). *The Effects of Autism on the Family.* New York: Plenum Press.

Stoneman, Z., Brody, G. H., Davis, C. H., and Crapps, J. M. (1988). "Mentally retarded children and their older same-sex siblings: Naturalistic in-home observations." *American Journal of Mental Retardation, 92,* 290–298.

Stoneman, Z., Brody, G. H., Davis, C. H., and Crapps, J. M. (1989). "Child-care responsibilities, peer relations, and sibling conflict: Older siblings of mentally retarded children." *American Journal of Mental Retardation, 93,* 174–183.

Tew, B., and Laurence, K. (1973). "Mother, brothers, and sisters of children with spina bifida." *Developmental Medicine and Child Neurology, 15,* 69–76.

Index